My Life: Woven with Threads of Black and Gold

Philip Nowell-Smith

Copyright © 2018 Philip Nowell-Smith

All rights reserved, including the right to reproduce this book, or portions thereof in any form. No part of this text may be reproduced, transmitted, downloaded, decompiled, reverse engineered, or stored, in any form or introduced into any information storage and retrieval system, in any form or by any means, whether electronic or mechanical without the express written permission of the author.

The views expressed in this work are solely those of the author and do not necessarily reflect the views of the publisher, and the publisher hereby disclaims any responsibility for them.

ISBN: 978-0-244-11164-9

PublishNation
www.publishnation.co.uk

Contents

Chapter 1 Up to the Age of Seven	1
Chapter 2 From the Age of Seven to Fourteen	8
Chapter 3 Fourteen to Twenty One	22
Chapter 4 1960's	47
Chapter 5 We Move to Somerset	67
Chapter 6 Summer Camps	81
Chapter 7 South Chard	86
Chapter 8 Mum and Dad	91
Chapter 9 Julia	94
Chapter 10 Teresa	96
Chapter 11 Ian	98
Chapter 12 Ruth and Hannah	102
Chapter 13 The Ukraine	106
Chapter 14 Mo's Illness	118
Chapter 15 Surprises	123
Chapter 16 Decision Time	126
Chapter 17 Our Golden Year	129
Chapter 18 New Zealand	132
Chapter 19 The Worst Day of My Life	134
Chapter 20 But Life Goes On	137
Chapter 21 My Health	143
Chapter 22 The Bucket List	145

Foreword

*The light shines in the darkness,
and the darkness doesn't extinguish the light.*
　　　　　　John 1:5 Common English Bible (CEB)

If you look at life, it's journey, and the people in it through the perspex of a kaleidoscope, there are colours. Colours make up the very picture of life, each colour weaving its way through the image to contribute to the final picture. Very much like a tapestry, some colours stand out, and some help build the picture. Gold stands out, especially against the black lines. In our lives Gold, representing the light in our lives, is not overshadowed in our lives by the black. A mother goes through so much pain to bring a life into the world, but once that new born is in her arms the physical pain is forgotten. Some pain lasts longer than other pain, but if you allow the light in, accept the joyous moments for what they are, appreciate the simple but awesome moments of God's multiple gifts, the darkness will not win.

Acknowledgements

Thank you, Tracy Clark, of PublishNation, for your constant advice and help.

To my daughter Ruth, thank you for all the hours you have spent editing and making improvements to the flow of the story.

I must also give a huge thank you for the invaluable prayer support to my pastor Brian Hilkene of Kings Church Quantocks; thank you Brian.

Finally, I want to give thanks to the Lord for encouraging me and leading me into a closer relationship with Him.

Chapter 1

Up to the Age of Seven

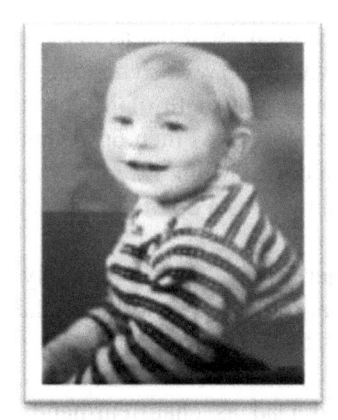

Me at 2 years old.

Both my mum and dad, Isabel and Jim, grew up in Swindon. More particularly Old Town, because the original village of Swindon was set on a hill overlooking the fields. When the Great Western Railway decided to establish their railway works at Swindon the new town quickly became established. My dad grew up at 88 Goddard Avenue in Old Town. Mum grew up at 14 Folkestone Road, also in Old Town.

Dad served a seven-year apprenticeship in the railway works to become a fitter, turner and erector, which meant as a fitter he was qualified to repair them. A turner was qualified to use machines working as a turner on a lathe, and also as an erector he actually built the locomotives.

I don't know much about mum's growing up. She was born in January nineteen hundred and five at 38 Hythe Road Swindon. I always thought the Nowell family home was in Folkestone Road and had never heard of Hythe Road until I examined her birth certificate.

Dad was eighteen months younger than Mum, and she married my dad on March the 30th at the age of twenty-two. In that period children left school at the age of fourteen and I can't imagine she would stay at home twiddling her fingers. Many girls were put into service as a domestic servant.

Dad was born on the sixth of November 1906, so he must have started his apprenticeship in 1920 but as his apprenticeship ended so did his employment with the GWR, so he found work in Basingstoke. They were married on the thirtieth of March nineteen hundred and twenty-nine. Mum's address was then 66 Avenue Road so I surmise that was the address of one of Mum's Aunts, where Mum was working she lived, and worked there as a domestic servant.

I am not sure where they set up home. My guess was with my Grandfather in Goddard Avenue. I do know that at one point in the early nineteen thirties they were both in service with a family in the Cotswolds' near Cirencester. Mum was employed as cook/housekeeper and Dad as chauffeur/handyman. It was in this period that my Uncle Harry, who was a pilot in the Royal Air Force, was flying over the Cotswold's and realised his sister and her husband were right down below. So, he landed his bi-plane in a field adjoining the house. Apparently, mum and dad were horrified Harry did this wondering if he would get into trouble. Harry's reply was Jim (my dad) would have to swing the propeller to start the engine and then nobody would know Harry had broken his journey. The only problem was that Harry had told dad to pull down on the propeller and step back smartly. I think that advice brought timidity and dad made a hash of swinging the propeller and the plane's engine failed to start. So, Harry had to phone his squadron and say he had to make an emergency landing, and could they send a mechanic to fix his plane's engine.

I know my mum became pregnant with twins, but she mis-carried and they had been married for nine years before I arrived on the twenty ninth of March nineteen hundred and thirty-eight. I was born at the Maternity hospital Kings Hill Road, Swindon. By this time dad was once again employed in the GWR railway works. The depression of the early 20's was over and engine construction was expanding.

Sometime before my birth mum and dad had bought a brand new semi-detached, three-bedroom house at one hundred and seventeen Oxford Road, in Stratton St. Margaret, Swindon. If I remember correctly, the price was three hundred and eighty-five pounds.

I was eighteen months old when the second world war broke out. As Swindon Railway works was one of the largest buildings in Europe, and was making tanks as well as engines and carriages, it was an obvious target for Nazi bombers, but the town got off very lightly, with nine bombs being dropped in fields surrounding the village. Fortunately, the only damage was a few frightened cattle and craters in fields. Between this incident there were several incidents but none of these raids caused human casualties, but that would change dramatically on the night of October twentieth, two bombs fell relatively harmlessly on Graham Street and York Road, but a third landed in Rosebery Street, killing 10 people, including a 12-year-old boy, all the dead were from four adjoining houses – numbers 115 to 118.

I do remember a Spitfire crashing on 7th December 1941. It landed in a tree at the intersection of Church Street and Ermine Street. The tree split down the middle but was still standing in 2004. The pilot was on a training flight and lost control and crashed into the tree and was killed instantly.

During this time mum was our local ARP Warden, and was given an official arm band that she had to wear when on her patrol making sure that the 'blackout' was enforced. Also, she was given a galvanized bucket and stirrup pump to tackle any fire that started. Some hope!

One day mum and I went for a walk across a field directly opposite our house. The field was separated by a dry ditch. I was just about to step down into the ditch when mum said quietly but firmly "Don't step down but step back." Even as a three-year-old I knew I had to do as I was told. When I had stepped back she explained to me that she had seen a snake which was just about to strike me. It was a viper and at my tender age a bite would probably be fatal. This wasn't my only experience with snakes. I was probably about six years old the next time I encountered a snake. Me and two or three mates were playing in the garden. At the bottom of the garden was the twin track main railway line from Paddington to Bristol.

Mum had told me NEVER EVER GO ACROSS THE RAILWAY LINE. But there was a gravel pit on the other side and loads of places to play hide and seek and Cowboys and Indians. So, we climbed down the cutting, crossed over the railway lines, and up the slope and through the fence. We were having a great time until I fell into the gravel pit. The problem was I couldn't swim and a snake, about four feet long, was swimming towards me. I immediately learnt to swim and scrambled out. Back through the fence, down the cutting, across the railway and up the slope into the garden. I went along the bath to the back door and knocked. Mum opened the door and saw the soaking, bedraggled boy standing in front of her. Her immediate action was to shout at me 'YOU'VE BEEN ACROSS THAT RAILWAY LINE' and clipped me around the ear. To me, mum didn't seem to understand that I couldn't swim or might have been bitten by the snake. It was years later that I realised besides Adders there were Grass snakes and Slow Worms, and much later that the only swimming snake is a Grass snake. Grass snakes, which grow to more than one metre (3ft) in length, live near water, mainly feeding on amphibians such as frogs, toads and newts.

But that was not the only worry that mum faced. At some point, in this stage of my life I contracted diphtheria and also tuberculosis. This meant having three operations on the left-hand side of my neck to remove infected glands. The last operation meant cutting open an earlier scar. Whether it was this or because I partially regained conciseness I don't know, but it meant that muscle contraction set in and the wound would not heal and mum had to apply hot kaolin poultices for three months before the neck healed. One time, when it came to change the dressing, it was stuck to my neck. Mum would fill a bowl with hot water and bathe the area until the water was no longer warm enough. I said to mum "go and get some more hot water" and before she came back I had taken hold of the corner of the dressing just like the nurses had done while I was in hospital. The things that stick in my memory is the fact that I learnt to write three times due to the amount of time spent in hospital during the war. Also, the operations were performed in a small hospital set on the edge of Savernake Forest. Once we were allowed out of bed we were allowed to play in the grounds. Three episodes remain with me. First, the gardener told us that a fox had killed some of his chickens. One day we spotted a fox and decided to chase it. There was no way we were going to catch it, but we found a clearing in the forest and a cricket match was in progress, so we sat and watched it. Didn't we get a telling off for being missing for the whole of the afternoon. On another occasion we noticed one of the lads was missing. He was very home sick, so we assumed he was on his way home. We started to follow him, but parked outside the main entrance was an Army ambulance with a member of the Women's Royal Army Corps who was just about to drive off. We explained, and asked if she could give us a lift in to town. Can you imagine that now a days? But she said, 'hop in' and we were off. Half way to the town we spotted him, so we asked the driver to stop and we frog marched the lad back to the ward. This time we were congratulated for bringing him safely back. The final episode was not so pleasant. We were playing in the spinney and as I ran through the shrubs and trees a branch whipped past my neck and tore three of my stiches out. It meant I was not allowed out to play for a couple of days. At that time there was no schooling provided so each time I went back to school I had to start over again, and although I was naturally left handed, mum insisted I write right handed. As a result, I now write and use a knife and fork right handed but use a soup spoon and dessert spoon left handed, and I am left footed. Sometime during this period, I contracted Diphtheria, which at that time was life threatening.

But I am getting ahead of myself. Mum took me to the doctors because I got so stressed every time the children caught the bus to school. I wanted to go too! So, the doctor wrote a letter to the school and as a result I started school at the age of three and a half, normally school age started at 5. The bus stopped right outside our front door and mum took me on the first day of term. Subsequently, mum put me on the bus and I must have crossed the road with all the other children and so into school. At least during the war there were very few cars on the roads. I only created a fuss at having to go to school once. That was when my uncle Len came to visit. Len was an officer in the RAF and a ground engineer maintaining the airplanes and mums' youngest brother. Needless to say, I went to school on the bus as usual.

The next thing I remember was Mum saying she had bought a second hand two wheeled bicycle and that she would teach me to ride it. She added that if I didn't master it on day one it would go back to the previous owner on day two, and by the end of the day I was riding up and down the pavement, and there after Mum spent the rest of the month worrying herself silly in case I crashed the bike and hurt myself or manage to get on the main road.

Soon after Dunkirk Dad was transferred to the Gloucester Aircraft works making aircraft and was conscripted into the local Home Guard in Stratton St. Margaret where he did every alternative night on duty. As there were bombing raids most nights the men spent a lot of sleepless nights fetching ammunition for the antiaircraft guns and tracking the planes but never opening fire. Unless there was a good chance of hitting a plane, you didn't disclose the location of the battery. So, dad went to work the next morning having been awake all night. During the day the battery was manned by regulars and dad never did have a good word for those who did the day duty and stayed in their beds all night. I guess that these men had survived Dunkirk and were on light duties.

After the panic of Dunkirk, dad was transferred back to the GWR engine works. At one point he was on nights and due to a shortage of man power, Dad had to go to the stores department to get a spare part. Unfortunately, with bad lighting and in a strange part of the workshop he took a step into nothing. He fell down a "Bosh hole" which was normally filled with caustic soda. It was used to dip engine axles into the caustic soda to clean off the grease and muck from the axle. During the day the covers had been removed and the Caustic Soda pumped out, but at the end of the day the covers were not replaced. Dad fell down and hit his chin on a ladder, he must have turned and presented the other jaw and he ended up in about three feet of sludge. His screams were heard and he was quickly helped out, but his trousers had disappeared in the Caustic Soda. He was rushed to the factory hospital where he was found to have both top and bottom jaws fractured and most of his lower teeth knocked out and imbedded in the palette of his mouth. Mum was called to his bedside and immediately fainted and fell under the bed. At the time my Auntie Flo, who was six years older than Mum, was the manageress of the refreshment rooms on Swindon railway station, and also my Gran was living in Swindon, and so what with neighbours' rallying around, Mum was supported during the coming months of Dad's slow recovery. The biggest problem was the reoccurring nightmares as he relived the accident. Mum would be wakened by his screaming and thrashing about the bed. His recuperation took a while and it was six months before he was allowed back to work. Whenever Auntie Flo had a day off she would come and visit us. One afternoon she took me to the pictures, I can't remember anything about the film except at the end the two stars embraced and kissed. It started to snow and gradually the snow increased and the couple began to fade away, hidden by the snow. My reaction was to speak out "Now the blasted snow coming" with my two fingers stuffed in my mouth all the while. It caused laughter all around and remained one of Auntie Flo's favourite stories to tell of me to all and sundry.

We caught the bus into Swindon one day in 1943. We sat on the top deck and I saw a group of British soldiers taking cover in a small clump of trees in the field next to the road. They were firing at some soldiers at the other side of the field, I just assumed they were Nazis' and got really worried. But they were Americans practicing for D Day. Outside on the grass verge military vehicles were parked nose to tail and soldiers were sleeping in and under the vehicles. We woke up one day and they had all disappeared, I knew not where.

At about this time, Mum began to consider the future. I was constantly under the doctor, and would Dad ever be able to go back to work. So, she decided that she would have to become the breadwinner for the family; this is how she related her decision, "After Jim had left for work one day I put a board up saying, 'House for Sale.' By the time Jim had come home, I had sold the house and bought a grocery shop in Swindon."

Chapter 2

From the Age of Seven to Fourteen

Age 11. Proudly wearing my American lumber jacket.

I don't know how my Mum explained her actions to Dad, but I do know he just accepted it. Mum had bought a two up, two down end of terrace leasehold property that had an outside toilet and no bathroom. We had gone from a new semi-detached, three bedroomed house with a bathroom upstairs and an outside toilet. The move from 117 Oxford Rd to 25 Tennyson St went straight over my head. All I know was that one morning I woke up in my usual bed and went to bed in my new home. The one thing that I noticed straight away was the HUGE air raid shelter at the bottom of the back garden. It must have been able to accommodate twenty or thirty people, which was a lot different from the Morrison shelter we had in the previous house. During March 1941 the Morrison shelter, named after the Home Secretary, was introduced. This was an indoor alternative to the Anderson Shelter, the corrugated iron construction that was half buried in people's gardens. The Morrison shelter was a large metal cage a little higher than a dining table. It had a hefty iron frame with a sheet steel top screwed together with chunky nuts and bolts. Underneath was a crude wire frame around the sides and a mattress on the floor. It was massive and angular and filled the dining room except for a space in front of the fire. But it did provide a good den for a five-year-old boy and his friends. I missed it in the new house. The front room of the new house had been turned into a shop with an 'L' shaped counter with shelves fitted to the walls behind. In the window was where the potato sack and other vegetables lived. But as I was only seven I was much more concerned with making new friends to play with because at the back of the small garden was a canal that had been filled in and grassed over and made an excellent place to play. Besides the huge air raid shelter in our garden, there was an even bigger one built on the 'Old canal' probably capable of accommodating a hundred people and was for the row of terraced houses that backed down to the canal on the other side. But in 1945 it was 'our den.' Then one day workmen came and demolished it, the war was over. Because I could readily get a supply of potatoes making a fire was one of our favourite pastimes. So, we spent a lot of time scavenging among the ruins for anything that would burn. One time I spotted something and ran over the rubble before coming to an enforced halt. My left shin had collided with an exposed metal reinforcing rod. My leg was bleeding quite badly but not enough to warrant me going in doors for mum to clean it and bandage it up, I just tied a handkerchief around my leg and got on with the job of baking the potatoes in the fire. Eventually it did dawn on me that as the metal rod was very rusty it could have been very serious, but I was lucky I guess. *Miracle*

One of the boys was a right cry baby and the gang had noticed his bike outside his front door. We nicked it and hid it in the bushes at the back of our street. As you can imagine, when he discovered his bike he went back indoors to mummy. She immediately summoned a policeman and we were rounded up and interrogated. At last we confessed and retribution was swift. The policeman took his belt off and used it to good effect. I didn't dare tell dad because he would have done the same. As I grew older I was expected to help mum in the shop, and my main job was weighing the potatoes. I do remember one occasion when the scale banged down heavily. One of the potatoes had an extra potato growing, so I promptly broke it off much to the horror of the customer. It was a huge learning scale for me. As a child I was told never to tell lies. One day an elderly lady came in and asked Mum if there was any tinned fruit. Mum said sorry. And I immediately said "Oh our mum! You should she what our Mum's got under the counter." The cat was out of the bag. I can't remember if the lady got a tin of fruit, but I learnt the difference between a lie and a white lie. Mum had to explain the lady lived alone and the tinned fruit under the counter was big tins of pears which was for families. When we had a case of mandarin oranges they would be for single people like the old lady.

We acquired a trade bike, so it became my job to go to the homes of customers and collect an order of what they wanted and then deliver it the next day after school and mum would give me a small amount of change in case I was given a pound note. I also remember that mum ran out of potatoes one day, so I had to take the bike to the local wholesaler for a fifty-six-pound sack. The weight sitting in the basket over the small front wheel made the bike very unstable, but I would not be beaten. I sat on the back mudguard, reached over the saddle and grasped the handle bar and peddle off home. I successfully reached home without incident, but I dread to think what would have happened if a policeman saw me. On another occasion I was sent to the local hardware store. For night time use we had a 'guzunder,' a chamber pot, which had become broken, I know not how, but I was sent to buy a replacement. I was asked if I wanted it wrapped, but I said no. Everyone in our neighbourhood used them so what was the problem. At this time, I was attending the local junior school just of Regent Street. It was an easy walk along the old canal, now filled in, then across the main road which was then relatively vehicle free. The teacher was a Mr. Rawlings and every day he would bring an apple into school, place it in his ink well and present it to the best student. He must have had an apple tree in his garden because I don't seem to remember a single day when the inkwell was empty. Also, in later years I realised he must have kept a record and made sure each child got an apple in turn.

The other events I remember at this time was sitting in the back row of the class and caught a fly, I proceeded to take the legs off one at a time before moving on to the wings. The girls at the next desk were horrified and soon Mr. Rawlings came to see what the disturbance was. My punishment was to sit in the middle of the girls' section of the class.

The boys and girls had separate play grounds. The toilets had been built to divide the two areas. Our favourite game as boys was to sally forth into the girls' section, grab one poor unfortunate girl and then drag her through the boys' lavatory screaming her head off. We would release her and then scarper before a teacher came to investigate what all the commotion was about.

During this time, I had to take sandwiches to school, which was ok. I absolutely loved beetroot sandwiches which were always eaten on the way to school and so I went hungry at lunch time. Mum was constantly running short of change, so I had to take an empty blue cloth money bag and a five-pound note and a list of coins mum wanted. Usually I would collect a pound's worth of copper, a pound of three pence pieces, a pound's worth in sixpences, a pound's worth of shillings and a pound's worth of florins. I knew that if I was robbed I could defend myself because I carried the bag over my left shoulder and if anyone did attack me I could hit them over the head. It never occurred to me that anyone could come up behind me and snatched the bag, such was the innocence of a child, but at that time five pounds was equivalent to a week's wage.

Mum was one of ten children and Granny Nowell lived in an Alms house in Old Town during the war. She was also from a large family so there was a large number of relatives in and around town which were very loyal to us as mum tried to make sure her business prospered. It must have done, because mum an dad bought a second-hand Austin 7, which dad use to drive all over Swindon delivering groceries to this relative and that one, and I would go with him. Occasionally the three of us would use our precious petrol coupons and drove to Weston Super Mare. It meant driving through Bath because I remember on the way back we went up this quite steep hill in Bath when the engine died. So, dad turned the car around and went back down the hill and tried again. The engine died in exactly the same spot. Dad understood that because the car was low on petrol the gravity feed couldn't pump the fuel uphill so once again he turned the car around, but this time instead of going down he started the engine and went up the rest of the hill in reverse. That wasn't the only excitement on that journey. On the way home we ran out of fuel and dad had a spare can with a gallon in it, just in case. As he was transferring it from the can to the car a policeman came up and asked if everything was ok. Yes, said dad and waited for the policeman to disappear. Apparently, dad was putting 'red petrol' into our car, which was very illegal as red petrol was for agricultural use only.

It was about this time that my Uncle Horace, his wife Aunty Madge and my cousin Anne came to see us. Horace was a fantastic swimmer They lived in Caversham, a suburb of Reading and he had a part time job working on an island in the River Thames helping people in and out of rowing boats and punts. One of his favourite pastimes was to dive off of the road bridge and whilst still submerged turn and swim upstream and watch the concerned onlookers when he didn't surface where they expected him to do so. However, back to the story. We all caught the train to Weston Super Mare and ended up at the Lido, an outdoor swimming pool. I couldn't swim but Uncle Horace persuaded me to climb up to the top of the water chute while he would be in the pool to catch me and he promised me the water wouldn't get up my nose. It did. My faith in him was totally destroyed and he and my parents just laughed at my discomfort. I was gutted and decided to run away. Which I did. As the time approached for the last train to Swindon the search for me got desperate and I was finally found about a mile away by the old pier at Birnbeck Island.

Horace had a severe stutter and was also double jointed and had 'elastic skin.' Which kept us kids in hysterics. To tie up his shoe lace he would walk up to a letter box, place a foot of the top and retie his shoe lace. He could put one hand on his shoulder and then pull the skin at his bent elbow about four inches out which meant he could never have a plaster applied to his skin, it always had to be bandaged. But his speech impediment got him into serious trouble as a young man. A motorist stopped and asked Horace "C....C...Can you direct me T...To..the, the, post office" Horace replied "Y......Y...Yes.. Sir It....It," when Horace suddenly got a clip around the ear, "Don't be so bloody cheeky." On another occasion when we visited them at their home in Caversham he took me and all my cousins out for a ride in his car. There were his daughters, Anne and Sara, two other cousins John and Jeremy and me. We came to a hill and Horace said, "There is so many in the car I don't think it will get up the hill." The car was moving at a walking place, so he wound down his window, got out of the car and pushed the car up to the top of the hill steering the car as he pushed. You can imagine our wonderment at his super human strength. It wasn't until I was in my teens and was taking a serious interest in cars that I realised that cars made in the 1930's had an 'advance and retard' leaver on the steering wheel to control the revolutions of the engine and thus the speed of the car. Auntie Flo would take me up to London on the train, and then we caught the tube to Edgeware Road. It was just a short walk to Madame Tussaud's. As we went in she noticed a policeman standing nearby, she was convinced it was a wax model and she wanted to show how I could spot the difference. She went up to him and said, 'I suppose you are made of wax' 'No, I'm real, can I help you?' She was dumb founded. At least two aunties took me to London and they also took me to Madame Tussaud's. I never did get to see any other of the wonderful sights of London.

At about this time I wanted to join the cub scouts. However, in order to join you had to join the local church group, Saint Marks. When Isambard Kingdom Brunel built the railway works he also built the houses for the workers. In addition, he built the Anglican Church and a Methodist chapel, a Playhouse and a Mechanics Institute. There was also a bath house because a lot of houses didn't have this luxury, and two swimming pools. The larger of the two was covered over in the winter and became a roller-skating rink. Finally, together there was a doctor's surgery, a dispensary, a hospital with a separate out-patient's department. Dad had sixpence (two and a half pence in today's money) deducted from his pay and it was generally believed that the National Health Service was modelled on the GWR Medical service. I joined the church but it very quickly became obvious that I couldn't sing, so dressed in my surplus and was given the job of swinging the incense as I preceded the vicar. St Marks was very high church, probably higher than a lot of Catholic Churches. I didn't care, it was my way into the cub pack.

Dad put his name down for a Hillman Estate car, because he had gone to school with one of the partners in the dealership. Mind you, it meant waiting a couple of years until dad finally got his brand-new car. However, he wasn't too happy with the fuel consumption and the garage had it back to do a road test. The foreman took the car out for a road test. The car was driven through a village halfway between Swindon and Marlborough. As he was driving around a left-hand bend in the village of Chiseldon he met a lorry coming the other way on the wrong side of the road. The foreman had just enough time to put the car into neutral and slide across the bench seat before the lorry hit our car. It was towed back to Swindon and Pressed Steel car works agreed to take the car into their works and repress it, such was the scarcity of cars at that time.

The time came for me to take my Eleven Plus exam. Swindon at that time had two grammar schools and my parents wanted me to go Goddard which was in Old Town. If I passed I could have a brand new bike. Mum and I debated and comprised. I wanted a racing bike with cable brakes, Mum as usual won! Needless to say, I didn't pass the all-important exam and went to the local Secondary School. Also, I didn't get the bike either. I took the exam the following year and again I failed, but I did get my bike, it cost twenty-one pounds, but I had to contribute a third of the cost. In the upcoming summer holidays, I cycled up to Caversham, via Marlborough where I joined the A4 main road from London to the West Country, which took me through Hungerford and Newbury and then through Reading. I stayed a week with Granny before making the return journey. I felt immensely proud of myself, having successfully completed the trip but also that Mum and Dad had trusted me to be sensible. I was twelve years old at the time.

During my second year I was introduced to Algebra. Surprisingly it made perfect sense to me, and the class would be set a page on questions that I solved in double quick time. I would sit quietly and the teacher would come and look at my work and he would say 'Well done, why don't you turn the page and try the next series of questions.' Which I did and ended up doing two years' work in one year. Another new subject was woodwork for the boys, but we had to make our own way to another Secondary school in Old Town. I realised that one of Mum's aunts lived very near to the school, so I made a point of calling in for a drink and a biscuit or a piece of cake after school. Her daughter had met a German soldier, who had been conscripted into the German Army and was stationed on the French coast. I was told that at some point he took his boots off and threw his rifle away and swam. Apparently, he was picked up and was brought to England. Nothing could have been further from the truth, perhaps Mum was a romantic. The German lad had come to England in the 30's because of the rise of National Socialism. He was interned on the Isle of Man as a matter of course at the outbreak of war in 1939. Eventually he was cleared and released back to mainland Britain where he served in the Pioneer Corps and later the Royal Artillery, met my Aunt and married her.

When I was thirteen I joined the Sea Cadet Corps, much more my cup of tea. We were issued with a proper seaman's uniform with a white top for summer and a blue serge jumper for winter use. We were also issued with a collar with the three white stripes around the edge and a black neckerchief which was worn under the collar and secured at the front of the jacket. Finally, we had a lanyard that was also worn under the collar and would be used to secure a knife or bosun's pipe. To round it off we were issued with a naval cap and a cap tally band with Sea Cadet Corps picked out in gold. We very quickly learnt to take the tally band off and replace it with "H.M.S." It made us look much more grown up especially if we would also wear a silk scarf around our neck and tucked into the front of the jacket. Then we would turn up the cuffs to hide the flash that identified us as Sea Cadets. I thoroughly enjoyed the four years I spent in the Sea Cadets. I became a Leading Seaman, (a corporal in the army) and I had three stripes on my arm, which represented three years in the sea cadets. In the Navy a stripe was awarded for four years good conduct. So, a 'three striper' was still only an Able seaman who had completed twelve years 'undetected crime' Everything was mirrored on the Royal Navy. We had a commanding office - the Captain, a First Lieutenant (known as number one) and four other Lieutenants. These were our divisional officers. My divisional officer was also the unit gunnery officer. He was responsible for teaching us to march and the various drills we would do with a standard issue .303 rifle used throughout the Second World War. During the day he worked in the GWR works just like my dad, but during the war he served on escort ships escorting merchant ships on artic convoys sailing up past Norway and Finland to Murmansk in Russia. He would relate that in the near constant gales the seas would break over the ships and as the seas hit the deck, superstructure, guns etc. it would immediately freeze and if not chipped off could result in the ship becoming top heavy and then it would turn upside down and sink. Anyone who fell over board would die of the cold within a couple of minutes. He didn't have a good word to say about Hitler and the Nazis. He would instruct us how to slope and order arms, present arms and fix or unfix bayonets. At the time there was a popular film about the American Navy about the Wavy Navy in which the sailors performed a series of drill movements without a single command being given. This was totally new to us but we wanted to do it too. He picked sixteen of us and eventually we could perform a drill sequence of about twenty minutes 'at the halt' and whilst marching. The most difficult manoeuvre was fixing bayonets whilst marching. The drill squad would attend fetes to give displays and collect donations for the unit. One display we did was to march around the tack at the Swindon Speedway arena before the races started. Another item the unit acquired was a two-pounder field piece. We constructed a version of the then famous gun run that featured in the military display at Earl's Court between the four division of the Navy, Plymouth, Portsmouth, Chatham and the Fleet Air Arm. We devised a miniature event, breaking down the gun into it four major components, the barrel, the wheels, the chassis and the ammunition trailer and taking these through the 'breach' in the wall and then over the 'river' by 'breaches boy' and fire a blank round and withdrawing the same way. In this way these two events raised huge amounts for the unit funds. Eventually the gun run had to be abandoned due to a lad who dropped the barrel on his foot, sustaining a broken toe. One evening the Skipper, as the Captain was known, turned up and let all us cadets in. There was about forty or fifty of us that night milling around waiting for the other officers to turn up. The skipper came out of his office and called me into his office. Apparently, no other officers could make it, so I was told to call the ships companies to form into their divisions. To do this I had to bring the ships company to attention and tell them to get into their respective divisions. When that had been accomplished I went to each division in turn and told the senior rating to 'inspect' the cadets and report that his division 'was all present and correct.' When all four had done this, I left the 'bridge' and went to the Captain's office and reported that the 'ships company was all present and correct for your inspection, Sir.' I did it. Phew! Shortly after this I was put in charge of 'stores' which meant that new lads joining had to come to me and I would issue a complete uniform to them and record just what had been issued. Every year the army cadets would go on camp as a unit. In the Sea Cadets, each cadet could choose from a list of courses available at different shore establishments. I always went to HMS Gamecock, a RNAS (Royal Naval Air Ship) station near Nuneaton in Warwickshire. We were given travel warrants where I would meet twenty or so other Sea Cadets from all over the country. This course specialised in packing parachutes and I got the technical badge, so I supposed I was now technically a Leading aircraft man. One afternoon each cadet in turn were taken up in a two-seater training aeroplane. I was told to look down at how small the cars were. So, I looked down and couldn't see anything except blue sky. Then I realised we were flying upside down. I was then asked if I would like to take the controls. Nervously I said yes please so the pilot told me what I had to do and he would be able to control my mistakes. I took hold of the joy stick and flew the plane watching the artificial horizon all the time, then he said to 'pull the stick back into your stomach and at the same time push the accelerator forward.' Then it was time to land. The pilot started the descent and pressed the button to lower the undercarriage. Immediately he radioed the control tower because he had one green light and one red light showing that one wheel had malfunctioned. We were told to fly as slow as possible and low over the control tower so the flight controllers could get a good look. The result was that it seemed to be ok but we should circle for a half hour to loose fuel. The pilot said I had a choice, I could take my chance and stay with the pilot who would attempt to land the aircraft, or I could bale out. I thought I might have the parachute that I had earlier packed and I certainly didn't trust my own effort, so I opted to take my chance with the pilot. All the emergency vehicles were at the edge of the runway and down we came. At the last moment he flew the aircraft and landed on one wheel until the aircraft had slowed down that the plane just sank onto to the suspect wheel. Everything was fine, just a faulty electrical contact.

Then came the ultimate experience. I had a phone call from the skipper during the Easter holidays. Dad was at work and Mum, who had just sold the shop, was working in a co-op store in Swindon. I had applied for a placement on a merchant ship and he was telling me that I had to report to the shipping offices in London that afternoon. I got my uniform on, packed a few clothes and my toilet bag and caught the next bus into town. I made my way to the co-op and told mum where I was going and could I have some pocket money. Next stop the Sea Cadets drill hall to see the skipper, collect my travel warrant and to find out where I had to go - Leadenhall Street and the head office of GSNC (General Steam and Navigation Company, where I had to sign on to the ships articles which made me an official member of the ship's company. I was told that I was not allowed to wear my uniform. A quick phone call to mum and a parcel was delivered to the ship next morning. We obviously had a better mail service back in the fifties. That day the last of the cargo came aboard and was stowed below in the hold. Apparently, we were taking supplies to the BAOR (British Army of the Rhine) and to various NAAFI (Navy, Army and Air Force Institutes). We set sail with the tide that evening to cross the North Sea and head for the River Rhine. I woke up once in the night for a loo trip. I stepped out of my bunk into about three inches of sea water. Nobody told me to make sure the plug was put into the sink to stop the sea water coming up the waste pipe as the ship rolled with the motion of the ship. I waited until the water flowed out, put the plug in the sink and spent the next couple of hours putting my towel on the deck, then ringing it out in the sink and pulling the plug out to get rid of the sea water. Eventually the floor was dry. My main task each day was to clean the ships bell, which hand not been touched for a year or more. It took a whole tin of brasso and the whole week to get it looking as it was supposed to.

Next morning, we entered the estuary and I saw my first strange sight. A small tanker with a raised bow and the stern was raised out of the water but to get from the front of the ship to the back meant a perilous journey as the deck in between was under water. The tanker was carrying fresh water to the ships in the estuary and because of the difference in the specific gravity of fresh water the salt water accounted for the fact that the tanker appeared more like a submarine than a ship.

We continued going up the Rhine, passing Emmerich am Rhein, to Duisburg. Düsseldorf, Krefeld and Cologne. At the first place I thought I would help open the hatches so some of the cargo could be unloaded. When we were tied up at one of the wharfs in London, as soon as the stevedores had finished they disappeared and the ship's crew would baton down the hatch covers. Apparently in Germany the Germans did everything. Then, when we were tied up, I would go ashore to see what there was to see in each of the towns. One of the sailors told me that the evenings would get quite cold and so he presented me with a tumbler three quarters full of Navy Rum saying, 'that will keep you warm.' This became the norm every time I went ashore and as I was only thirteen, I never ever told my mum of my drinking habit when I was in Germany.

When my parents first bought the shop, every Friday the tin bath that hanged on a nail in the yard was brought indoors and placed on the rug in front of the hearth. I would be bathed first and then sent off to bed, next mum would have her turn and finally Dad would take a long soak to get all the dirt and grime off. One of the first improvements they made was in the kitchen. They had a bath installed and a Beeston boiler fitted to heat the water with anthracite. What luxury!

It seemed to me that bath night was still Friday. On other days a table top would be lowered to cover the bath. But mum would use the bath to wash the bedding by getting in the bath with the water and soap powder and walking up and down over the bedding. The next thing they did was to have the yard enclosed with a glass roof so we didn't have to go outside to the toilet.

In 1954 Mum and Dad bought a lovely house in Watchfield. It was a three-bedroom detached house standing in about a half-acre of garden. The landing was so big there was room for a single bed and a huge walk in airing cupboard, and a bathroom. There was a huge living room with a big square bay window overlooking the front garden. Off this room was a conservatory and the attached garage was behind the kitchen. Off the hall was the separate dining room. There was a second garage set amongst three horse chestnut trees and in the rear garden there was a huge beech tree. Finally, there was a flowering almond tree and an apple tree.

The house in Watchfield.

Dad and I, taken when I was 13 years old.

Chapter 3

Fourteen to Twenty-One

Each morning we would all drive into Swindon. Dad would park the car at the shop, then walk to work and I would cycle to school while Mum ran the shop. After school I would continue to call on customers for the grocery order and then deliver them the following day. One of these was Mrs. Warren, who lived in Theobold Street at the time when Mum bought the shop in 1944. Now she was living with her daughter and son-in-law in Groundwell Road. One day in the Easter holidays I cycled over in the morning to pick up her order and ended up staying for a couple of hours. Staying with her were three children she had met on Bournemouth beach who were holidaying with their parents. Mrs. Warren, better known as Auntie B (Beryl) was a dedicated match maker. I was introduced to Clive, Maureen and Margaret Hill who lived in Cardiff. Their parents and the three children were on holiday in Bournemouth and met Mrs Warren on the beach there. Clive and Margaret were stripping paint in the front room while Maureen and I were put to work in the dining room. I had the blow lamp and it was made clear to me that I spent more time burning Mo (Maureen) than paint. The next day I went back with the groceries and spent the whole day there. On the Saturday Auntie B treated us to a visit to the theatre, I can't remember what we saw but I do know we were up in the 'gods.' The next day they caught the train back to Cardiff; Auntie B made Mo promise that she would write to me when she got home. The next time I saw Auntie B, I had to make the same promise. Eventually Mo did write to me, but it was made abundantly clear that she had written only to fulfil the promise. The letter ended with 'You don't need to reply if you don't want to. Soon we became pen pals. I was fourteen and Mo was thirteen. At that time girls who were called Maureen would shorten their names to Mo after the American tennis player Little Mo Connolly.

Eventually I was nagged by Auntie B to write back to Mo. Gradually we became pen pals and were writing to each other once a week.

During this time, I took the thirteen plus exam which I did pass and so in September I went to a secondary technical school, where the options were brick laying, metal working or shorthand and typing. This was my choice, and I excelled in typing and could touch type at thirty words a minute. Shorthand was a bit more of a problem. I can remember the first six shorthand symbols \, \, l, **l**, /, /. Each was either a light stroke or a heavy stroke. The problem was with fourteen girls in the class I could easily copy out the homework before lessons started. As a result, all I remember is the heavy upright stroke represents 'day.' Also, now I was fourteen and beginning to show an interest in girls. In particular Julia who lived in Highworth and Julie who lived in Swindon. They quickly became inseparable, but I took a shine to Julia. But it didn't last long.

The Technical school syllabus was to last two years, but at the end of the first year my English teacher, who happened to by my Auntie Freda, wrote in my school report that I had no knowledge of the English language. Mum was furious and made arrangements for me to move schools. In the meantime, us boys might have been influenced by the fact that none of us liked her. When lessons finished for the day, we would lift the bonnet of her Austin Seven and take the rotor arm out and chuck it away. Or course the car wouldn't start so Freda would phone her garage who quickly discovered what was wrong. A quick trip to the garage for a replacement rotor arm and she was on the way home. This happened regularly once a week and the mechanic always brought with him a spare rotor arm.

If this had any effect on my school report I don't know, but Mum went ballistic. She took me out of school and enrolled me into a small independent private school for boys, and straight into a two year O-level course. We were terrible. Our Math's teacher was a lady who had a very high-pitched voice who constantly shouted at us so much that the head master's reaction was to cane the whole class. We had to line up outside his study in alphabetical order. At the time my surname was plain 'Smith' so I was quite happy to be at the back of the queue. I reasoned his arm would be a bit tired by the time he got to me. The French teacher was not much better. He was susceptible to being led up the garden path and we boys were very good at leading him there. We also made a point of passing a pen from someone in the front row to the back row. When the time came to copy something into our exercise book the boy would just sit there looking helpless. Eventually Sir would ask why the unfortunate boy was not writing up his notes. "Someone has taken my pen, Sir" so 'Sir' would lift up the lids of adjoining desks looking for the missing pen. He would repeat this at every desk in the room by which time the missing pen had mysteriously turned up with its owner.

The head organised a holiday to Blankenberge in Belgium, so we took the opportunity of walking through the town smoking. One day we met the head coming the other way, so we hid our cigarettes and he said, "Don't worry, I know you're smoking." The next day we didn't bother to hide our cigarettes. This time he tore a strip of us, so we came to the conclusion that the day before he had backed a winner on the horses and the next day he had lost. The challenge on the way home was to smuggle something back into England without declaring it. I bought a small bottle of perfume and strapped it to my ankle and successfully got it in undiscovered. I was fifteen at the time and became a prefect. One of our responsibilities was to supervise the younger boys across the road. The bonus was we would get to meet up with the girls at an adjacent private school, chatting up one girl in particular, Diana Fluck who became Diana Dors.

Mum and dad bought a touring caravan which they sited at Radcot near Lechlade on the upper reaches of the River Thames and we would spend our weekends there. The field was on an island and there were about nine caravans sited there permanently. Dad and I would spend time fishing for chub, roach and eel. The only one I didn't like eating was roach, they tasted very much of mud. Eel had to be skinned. This was done by nailing it to a post with a nail in the head and cutting the skin right around just behind the fins and then cutting the eel into cutlets and frying on the barbecue Also, I would also spend a lot of time swimming. The main channel was kept free of weeds but the other stretch was very weedy, but in spite of this I would swim right around the island, a distance of about two miles. I started at the bottom of the island where the back-water channel re-joined the main river and I would swim upstream and turn into the back stream. My logic was I could use the current as by now I would be getting tired, also if my feet got entangled in the weeds I would keep them still and as I drifted on the current my legs would become free. In time we also bought a small boat which we had first seen at the boat show held in Olympia. It was just nine feet long with a beam of four feet and made of aluminium with a small outboard motor. Under each seat were flotation aids so even if it became holed it would not sink. Dad constructed a framework that fixed to where the row locks were fitted and then he had to make one in the bows and another two in the stern. The canvas boat cover could then be placed over the framework. To make it totally enclosed two side canvas' were tied on to the framework. The next job was to make four brackets, two of which went from the seat in the bows and the middle seat, and the other two from the middle seat to the stern seat. To these were added planks of wood and cushions. We were all set to make our way down the River Thames to Reading. Each night we would take the boat out of the water and make our beds up, get a hot meal cooked on a paraffin pressure stove and bed down for the night. A distance of sixty-two miles and twenty locks each way. It was a great 10 days and the weather was kind as well.

By now Mo and I were writing to each other on a regular basis and we even conspired together to go on holiday with our families to a Butlin's holiday camp in North Wales. Both families drove up and at one point we stopped and asked directions of the local Welsh who obviously were winding us up, saying they didn't speak English. However, we eventually found our way. Someone had found out the ruse. It certainly wasn't me or Mo, I suspect it was Mo's younger sister. Clive had also brought his girlfriend. Any way we all had a good time, our parents got to know each other, and Clive and his girlfriend went riding every day.

Mum was happy. At the end of the two years I passed my English language exam, Maths and Geography. I failed the History exam, one of the questions was to describe the events of the 1715 Scottish rebellion. I knew if off by heart, the only problem was I wrote about the 1745 rebellion.

Towards the end of the summer holidays I had decided I had had enough of school and sat the entrance exam to become a clerk in the railway works, which I passed. However, as my O levels were a bit disappointing I was persuaded to go back to school on Saturday mornings and retake History and English Literature and I managed to pass in History. I started work as a junior clerk working in the AM Shop, this was the Machine shop with lathes of all sizes, both small and large that could accommodate a complete crankshaft for a locomotive. The office I was in had a chief clerk and six clerks. My main task was to write out privilege railway vouchers that could be changed for tickets at the railway station. Also, if one of the workers needed to leave work for any reason he had to hand in his 'pass out' at the gate so his wage could be adjusted accordingly. Pretty boring really. One day I was persuaded to back a horse. It was the two thousand Guinee's, I tried to explain that I didn't know the front of a horse from the back. But it wouldn't do. I looked at three different national daily newspapers and each one gave a different favourite, so I backed them ten pence each way and they came in first, second and third and I won the equivalent of two weeks wages. My modest stake won me nearly ten pounds and there and then I decided that that was the last time I would back a horse. I had my bet and I have never betted again, at least I came out on the winning side.

My Uncle Harry, who at this time I had tremendous respect for, was Director of Personal at the Air Ministry and had arranged for me to go to RAF Hornchurch in Essex for a medical for flying duties. He said to me that he knew "I would fail because I wore glasses, 'but it would stand me in good stead' when you go for a ground commission."

A/Com H.E. Nowell, CB, OBE.

I would have liked to have got a commission in the RAF. I had three uncles and two cousins commissioned in the RAF, so it was a family tradition. However, would I have ever known if I deserved it or had it been handed to me on a plate. I couldn't take the chance.

My first choice was as a ship's writer in the Royal Navy. That meant signing on for twelve years, which I thought was to long of a commitment, so I settled on the Army. I signed on for three years on the sixteenth of December nineteen fifty-five at the age of seventeen and three quarters. I was immediately sent home 'on unpaid leave' and told to report to the RAPC (Royal Army Pay Corps), or within the army known as the 'Rape And Plunder Corps,' on the third of January nineteen fifty six at the training battalion in Devizes.

I had been earning three pounds a week and had had to pay Mum a pound a week towards my keep and buy my own clothes when I worked for the Great Western Railway. As I was a regular soldier my starting pay was three pounds and three and sixpence a week (£3.175). I was immediately better off because the army clothed me and fed me. Whereas if you were conscripted the rate was One pound and eight shillings (£1.40) a week.

The other advantage was I got to choose what branch of the army I served in, hence I was able to choose the Pay Corps. As I had chosen to make the army my career I was automatically promoted to substantive corporal on the 16th of December 1956, and then five years later, if I had stayed in the Army I would have been promoted to substantive sergeant. I would have been still only twenty-three years old at the time of my promotion to the rank of sergeant. I would have taken a correspondence course, which the Army would have paid for, and trained to be a charted accountant. So by the time I was thirty I would have been qualified and I would have to choose whether to stay in as a Captain, and make the Army my career, or come out and find a private firm where I could continue my career. National Service was still in effect and about 200 recruits turned up every month for twelve weeks basic training. Both regular recruits and national service men were treated exactly the same, being constantly bullied, shouted at and having our kit thrown out of our lockers because it 'wasn't up to standard.' We had two pairs of boots, one we wore every day and a 'best' pair that had to be 'bulled.' This involved heating the handle of a dessert spoon over a candle and then rubbing it over the toe cap of the boot to smooth out all the bumps on the leather. When that had been done satisfactory we then had to put some polish on a rag and spit on the toe cap and rub it in and polish it till you could see your reflection.

Our days were filled with marching drills and going on five-mile marches with full kit over the chalk hills of Wiltshire. There was a bayonet drill and then disaster struck. I was negotiating the assault course when I fell and damaged my knee, which meant I couldn't March or do any of the drills. So, at the time everyone was out on the square learning the various drills with a rifle I was in the barrack room working on my best pair of boots. When they came into the barrack room they would say 'we learnt to present arms or fix bayonets' or whatever had been the drill for the day. I would say I can do that. I would get my rifle out of the locker and do it without banging my feet up and down. The corporal in charge of us got wind of it and checked me out and then spoke to the sergeant. As a result, I was not 'back squadded' but kept my place in the platoon. *Miracle* Therefore, I passed out with my mates. The only difference was that I sat in the grand stand with Mum and Dad, who had come down for the passing out parade. Before we left the training battalion we were 'invited' to say where we wanted to be posted. I put in for Belize, a small country in South America, but I realised I wouldn't get that because of my medical classification, so I was posted to the RAPC regimental pay office for the Royal Electrical and Mechanical Engineers which was also in Devizes. I was gutted. I wanted to see a bit of the world. The only bit of excitement that we had was when there was a fire drill in the middle of the night. One of the men in our barrack room worked in the regimental office so we were forewarned. All twenty of us decided that we would sleep through the alarm which was about two in the morning. Of course, we heard it, but we were all tucked up fast asleep when the RSM (Regimental Sergeant Major) and the Orderly Officer came into the room and banged on the end of the bed shouting their heads off 'what are you lot doing here, didn't you here the fire alarm?' As one we all said 'No, Sergeant Major.' One bright spark said there must have been something wrong with the fire alarm. One of the lads had shorted the wire out so it didn't work, but they were not to know that, so the two officers agreed it was too late now, so we got to go back to sleep. We didn't hear any more about it, but the fire alarm was repaired, so our excuse worked.

Six week later I was sent on two weeks embarkation leave, the end of which I was to report to the RAPC depot at Ash Vale, Aldershot. I had been there for about three weeks, when on one weekend home, Uncle Harry arranged for me to go up to London for the evening to watch the Royal Tournament. I thoroughly enjoyed it and caught the last train back to Ash Vale. However, I had fallen to sleep and woken up at Aldershot which meant a four-mile hike back to Ash Vale. I found out there were six of us going out to Benghazi in the province of Cyrenaica in Libya, and therefore no alcohol. Therefore, I went into Aldershot every evening for the last six days in 'Blighty' and drank six pints of 'black and tans' (each black and tan was half a pint of Guinness and half a pint of brown ale). I also ordered a tot of rum in each glass. Then I tried to walk the four-mile journey along the white line back to camp. By the time I arrived at the guard room I was sufficiently sober to escape being detained. As I was a regular and the rest of the party were National Servicemen I would be in charge and given two stripes to put on my arm. It was made clear that the promotion was only 'acting and unpaid' so I didn't worry too much when I failed to see an officer and failed to order my squad to 'Eyes right' and salute him. The worst he could do was to put me on defaulters when I would be back to a private. He couldn't even do that, we were on the way to the airport. Can't remember how we flew, but I guess it was on a Tristar aircraft operated by the RAF. Certainly, our kit weighed more than twenty kilos, more like double. The airport at Benina was about eighteen miles south of Benghazi on a mountain plateau known as the Jebel Akhdar.

Our destination was the headquarters of the troops in Cyrenaica and was originally built by the Italians. The District Pay office had their offices on one side of the square, our barracks were on the opposite side, and the headquarters staff and the Generals office on the third side opposite the main entrance. On the fourth side was a mosque and a NAFFI canteen. We were quite a small unit of about forty, housed in five rooms of eight men all interconnected with an open passage way passing through. I chose the furthest from the end of the passage way and a bed next to a window. The walls were about two-foot thick, so it was quite comfortable, warm in winter and cool in summer. The first surprise was the next draft to arrive. Two of the new chaps kneeled down at their bedside so say their prayers. The other five and I didn't say anything but next day said, 'we'll soon sort them out,' forgetting that they had come straight from the ten-week training battalion. In fact, it was exactly the opposite. Everyone in the army had to have a 'religion.' The two Christians were a Methodist and a C. of E. I had put my religion down as C. of E., another was Church of Scotland. Of the remaining two, one was an atheist and the other agnostic. The final chap was a Jew. We would spend hours discussing 'religion' with the two Christians and it led to us taking part in daily readings and meeting once a week to discuss what we had read in the week. Each day we had to record what verse had spoken to us that day and then when we met together we would name the verse of the week. On Christmas Day it fell to us in the District Pay Office to mount a three-man guard with a corporal in charge. There were two church services arranged, one for Roman Catholics and a combined service for Anglicans and free church personnel. About six months after my arrival there were enough volunteers who were willing to stand guard for a couple of hours so that even those who were on guard were able and did in fact go to church on Christmas Day.

Soon after I arrived the British and French forces invaded the Egyptian Suez Canal zone. This meant there were some additional security measures imposed. The treaty arrangements allowing British troops to be stationed in Libya meant that these stations could not be used as a staging post for use against other Muslim countries. There was, however, a perceived danger to individual soldiers being attacked. The main threat was from extremists. In Tripoli soldiers leaving barracks had to be in groups of a minimum of three, one of whom was armed. Cyrenaica was much more pro-western, and we had to be in groups of two and we were not armed. At the entrance to the headquarters' barracks security was increased. The orders published were that guards were to search all vehicles, both civil and military. As the majority of military vehicles were driven by local Arabs it meant that we had to search them. There was a twofold problem, no extra men were allocated for the task and one of the places where explosive might be hidden was the spare tyres. Again, there was no training or tools to do the job. So basically, we the British Tommy just ignored the instructions. The general was apparently horrified, because he issued new orders which emphasised that vehicles MUST BE SEARCHED. The next day the orders were carried out exactly. Every car was to be searched. The queue became so long that day, that the general's car, which was so far back in the queue, never got to the main gate and the General did not get to his office that day. Strange really, fresh and more sensible orders were issued, like how to examine the inside of the spare wheel of a fifteen hundred weight lorry, with no tools to accompany this. Thus, this was also ignored. It was a different kettle of fish for the Veterinary corps. There was a small detachment who regularly operated dog patrols around army fuel dumps and ammo stores. Again, these were three men patrols with their war trained dogs which meant the dogs had been trained to attack the 'enemy' by going for the throat which meant to kill on command. These guards were increased in size which meant the soldiers were doing six guards a week in addition to their dog training during the day. One day I was on guard duty when a dog patrol passed by the main gate to guard the fuel dump. Their training included one of them dressed up in very smelly Arab clothing. There were always Arabs hanging around the main gate hoping to get a hand out from a friendly person. The result was spectacular, the dogs got the scent and were all straining at the leash and the soldiers leaning back and digging the heels of their boots in to the road surface being literally dragged along the road. The war in Suez lasted only six weeks but before it was over the dog handlers were like zombies through lack of sleep and inventing ways of keeping awake during the night. One group decided to play Russian Roulette and one soldier was eventually shot and killed. The accused was brought to the guard room at our barrack. The guy was in such a state all guard commanders had to be taught how and when to administer another injection to keep him subdued. I was just glad I was still a private then, but as a unit we also got additional places to guard. One was the NAFFI store compound. Ordinarily, this was guarded by locally employed Arabs, but now these were backed up by a military picket of three men, with just one soldier patrolling, armed with a pick axe wooded shaft, while the other two slept. The Arab night time security had their own 'gaffer', who I found fast asleep in a little hut. I immediately woke him up and told him to do his job properly and then laid down and promptly went to sleep myself. Then there was a huge explosion that sounded is if it were right outside. I was convinced that somebody had blown up the stores compound I was supposed to be guarding. I rushed out and checked the whole perimeter, but everything was peaceful. But I didn't get back to sleep that night. I later learnt that a kerosene dump had been blown up. But on the whole, this 'little war' didn't affect us, and we were still allowed to go into town and the Arab Suk.

    The day would come in November 1956 when I was promoted to full corporal. I immediately had to go on a two-week weapons training course, so far, I had only handled a Lea Enfield .303 rifle. Now I was introduced to a .45 revolver, a sten gun (a machine gun that came with a tripod mounting) and a sten gun, which used 9mm ammunition. The sten gun had been developed for the D day landing, and by using nine-millimetre ammunition could use Nazi ammo. I had to learn how to strip, clean and reassemble them and fire them. For this the target was a silhouette of a man made out of plywood, known as a 'slim jim.'

With the revolver I couldn't even hit the target, but I became a marksman with the sten gun. I don't know if it was true, but it was reckoned to have cost ten shillings (fifty pence) to make. It had a magazine of 32 rounds and could be used for a single shot or fully automatic when it fired at the rate of six hundred rounds a minute.

My pay went up to seven pounds seven shillings a week (£7.35) a week, and I would be a guard commander. It was my duty to stay awake all night and to supervise the rotation of the guard's stint of two hours on and four off, when they could sleep on one of the beds in the cells if there were one empty. I had taken my jacket off and it was draped over my chair. I was sat on the table leaning against the wall asleep. In the chair was my one and only prisoner keeping me company, when two military police walked in with a drunk to be locked in the cells. I slept through the whole procedure, and after my prisoner had deposited the drunk in a cell, signed the receipt and the police had gone, he woke me up to tell me what had happened. If he hadn't been quick witted I would have been in the cells and facing a general court martial. It was also fortunate that I had taken my jacket off because the 'Red Caps' had assumed I was a private and the prisoner was the guard commander. Whilst I was stationed in Benghazi one soldier decided to desert. He must have done his research because he headed for the port and boarded a ship that was just about to depart for the United Kingdom. Apart from that one incident life was all good. We would get up at whatever time we liked, get dressed and run down the stairs and stop at the NAFFI and get a breakfast roll with a couple of fried eggs in it and a mug of tea and take it into the office. We called everyone by their first names including my WO2 (Warrant Office second class) Ernie. Only WO1, Rice and the officers were addressed as Sir.

The army taught me to sail a fourteen-foot cutter in Benghazi harbour sailing in and around the bombed-out wrecks that had been sunk in World War 2. I remember we were going so fast that I had my toes under the bar on the keel housing and my upper legs on the gunwale hanging on to the jib sheet with my head panning over the water. I eventually passed and became qualified to take on the duties as skipper. They also taught me to ride a horse. This was another part of the vets' jobs - to manage the stables. In addition to the horses in the stables a lot of the officers had also brought their hunters with them from the UK. First, I had to learn how to mount and dismount. Then the four of us in the school learning to ride were told too 'walk on'. We walked our horses out of the riding school. It seemed to me that my horse was going slower than the rest and was falling behind. Sure enough, when we got to the school ground, which was a large oval ring surrounded by a very high wall, the corporal instructor told me to catch up. I dug my heels into his flanks, and immediately the horse bolted for the wall. The corporal shouted to me 'lay flat on the horse's back with your feet straight out in front.' I did as I was instructed and the next moment I was standing straight upright and the horse standing on his front feet and his back legs high in the air. Once he was on all fours, he re-joined the school and started going slow again. I certainly wasn't going to kick him, so I just clicked my tongue and we were off again straight for the wall. This time I was told to lean forward and put both arms around the horse's neck. This time the horse reared up on his front legs and I was left holding on for dear life. The class lasted an hour and I survived, I beat the horse and I never had any trouble with him after that. Once we were proficient at riding we were allowed to follow the hunt. As I said a lot of officers had brought their horses from the UK. These were English hunters whereas the majority of horses in stables were local Arab which were more suited for the local terrain. We would hunt the local desert fox over the Jebel Akhdar (meaning Green Mountain) and down the side of dry wadis (water valleys). As these were very steep descents we were told to let go of the reigns and lean back on the horse's withers or get off and walk the horse down. Or course the fox never played fair. On the one occasion that a fox was caught the Master shot the fox with his service revolver.

One time my pony was intent on getting to the front of the pack and I was told in no uncertain terms 'you there, get back in your place.' The only way I could respond was to pull a reign hard left and bring his nose to my left foot. The result was he couldn't see where he was going and had to stop. In the process I came off but managed to hold on to the reigns. I managed to get one foot in the stirrup but went straight over the horse landing on the floor on the other side of the horse because he felt my weight, and he was away. Finally, next time

I was successful and re-joined the hunt. On one occasion I went out for a ride, and everything went well as I left the stables but when I let him control the direction he turned straight back towards the stables. At the third attempt I decided to head back and one of the vets took the saddle off and the horse had a huge sore under the saddle. The Arab groom got a big telling off.

Then the army sponsored me to go on a lifesaving course down on the beach. I passed but it was one of those occasions I never volunteered for in the Army. The commanding officer arranged for us to 'go on an exercise' with a couple of lorries brought in and tents for the exercise. We were supposed to be working in a moving in the desert situation I guess, re-enacting the desert situation in World War 2 between Rommel's Africa Corps and Montgomery's 8th army backward and forwards across North Africa. In actual fact is was an excuse for us to let our hair down because we camped right next to the Sea. But the water had to be deemed safe to swim in and that was down to me. I had a length of rope attached to me and I had to assess the current. I knew if I had deemed it unsafe I would be strung up from the nearest tree. I therefore declared it safe and when everyone was in the sea swimming, I had to remain on shore, with a rope attached in case someone got into difficulty.

My time seemed to be so full with one thing or another. I took to going to the company sergeant major and saying that I thought I had a guard duty soon, I'm available on Tuesday of next week. Looking back, it sounds audacious, but he was always obliging. I would occasionally hire a bicycle and ride out to the local countryside, find a shady date palm to sit against and pick fresh dates from the tree, delicious, never have they tasted so good. On other occasions I would take a look at the local zoo. I also enjoyed taking a taxi into town invariably an American 'Chevy' with column change and front bench seat. One took one's life in ones' hands. Arab drivers would drive with the gas pedal to the floor, approach a corner, put the car into neutral then engage the gear when the car had negotiated the corner. Not good practice or the safest way to drive. On occasions there was babysitting when married personnel had 'do's' in the mess. This could even extend to the USAF (United Stated Air Force) who had a base nearby.

They lived like 'lords.' They sent an aircraft every other day to Italy just to bring in fresh milk, whereas we British had to rely on evaporated milk. Mind you it made very good rice pudding but didn't taste right in tea. Then my section sergeant and his wife took a leave break in Cyprus. They lived in a 'private hiring' in the village about half a mile away for the barracks. He asked me if I would like to move in. Apparently, private hiring's couldn't be left empty. There were a couple of alarm clocks in the apartment, so I set one and place it in the kitchen and the second one by my bedside. My thoughts were the kitchen alarm would wake me up and then I could have a fifteen minute lay-in until the second alarm went off fifteen minutes later. It worked well until one day neither of them woke me up, the first thing I heard was the local Catholic church literally next door started to ring the church bells. I jumped out, threw my clothes on and ran all the way to the office, arriving about two minutes late. One time, four of us hired a car from a local Arab for the day. We set out early and drove along the coastal highway eastward towards Cyrene. When Jesus was condemned to be crucified the Romans got a man from Cyrene to carry the cross for Jesus. Apollonia was once a thriving port serving Cyrene but at some time most of the port disappeared under the sea. We had brought flippers and face masks with us and spent a super hour or more swimming in doors of houses and then out of the windows. And then on another occasion we drove to Barca, another Roman settlement. When we got there one of the lads asked me if I could teach him to drive. As we were off road I deemed it safe to let him have ago. The car started with a number of jolts along a grass track. Everything was going fine until we saw a big stone sticking up above the grass. Instead of going around it he put the stone right between the left and right-hand wheels. The stone hit the sump nut and knocked it off. We were going nowhere unless we got help. Fortunately, there was an army base nearby. The 5th Battalion Royal Tank Regiment sent out a 10 Tonne lorry to tow us into the base. The driver got a chain out, fixed it to the tow hook on the lorry, the other end was attached to the front spring. The length of chain meant that I was following the lorry that was only six feet in front me, and all I could see was the bit of road under the lorry. I'm sure the lorry driver forgot he was towing me. By the time we got to the army base I was a completely exhausted wreck having had to be so concentrated on missing potholes and the sudden braking of the lorry. The vehicle mechanics took the sump off and told us that as it was made of aluminium the sump would have to be 'Brazed together and it was going to be a long job.' It eventually was finished, and it was after midnight when we got back to barracks only to find the owner of the car waiting for it. We didn't say anything about the sump but we must have got a story together. I think it was on the drive back to Benghazi that we came across a group of Libyan men dancing around and generally fooling about in the middle of the road. I realised it was Ramadan and they had been fasting all day and then spent the evening drinking alcohol – despite being strictly forbidden according to Muslim law.

If we ever journeyed into the desert and we saw a pile of stones pilled one of top of the other it signified a mine field. We didn't dare to go any further. Fighting between the British and the Nazi forces ended in Cyrenaica in November 1942 and the minefields had not been cleared when I was there in November 1956. Young Arab children were quite often brought into the military hospital with a leg having been blown off because they had stepped on a mine. Near the Egyptian border a lorry went south into the desert to recover a single seater fighter plane downed in world war 2. It had laid undisturbed for seventeen years or so. The pilot was still sat in the cockpit perfectly preserved due to the dry atmospheric conditions. But as soon as the cockpit cover was removed the mummified remains just collapsed into dust.

It might seem that all I did was enjoy myself. I did, but I had to work as well. In the summer period work started at 07.30 until 13.00. Afternoons were free.

In winter we wore BD (Battle Dress) and worked from 09.00 until 17.00 with a lunch break in between. Even in winter temperatures could get up to 25 degrees or so but fell away quickly as the sun went down. So, when we were on guard duty we would wear our pyjamas under our BD then our great coat and scarf and still freeze.

There was one soldier in another unit who was desperate to get out of the army. Every day when he saw a scrap of paper on the floor he would pick it up, unscrew it, smooth it out and read it. Then he would screw it up again and throw it away saying, 'that's not it.' He kept this up for about three months when he was sent to the hospital where he continued his ritual. The phycologists tried everything to trip him up but to no avail. Eventually he was summoned to a medical panel where it was decided that he was medically unfit for military service. The senior medical officer signed his discharge paper and gave it to the soldier. He looked at it, snapped to attention and said, 'Thank you sir, that's it,' saluted, turned about and marched out a free man.

In early March the CO paraded the whole unit and had a rant. He told us that we were all fully trained as both soldiers and clerks, so we should be able to use our initiative rather than having to resort to relying on the officers and senior NCO's; and in a couple of weeks later we would be approaching the end of the financial year. New tax cards would have to be prepared for 15,000 personnel. It was a job that had to be done by an NCO. That meant me and a lance corporal, Wally Smith.

On the Saturday I said to Wally "Are you game to go into the office and make a start on these records?" 'Yes' he said. So, we went over to the office, checked in with the duty clerk. There was always someone in the office twenty-four seven and he duly logged us in his report, the time we entered and the time we left. We took our meal breaks, lunch and supper, and left at about ten o'clock. We repeated this on the Sunday, but we had to work through the night until about three a.m. into Monday morning. We went back to the barrack room and got a couple of hours sleep and were back in the office at the normal time.

The CO had been in the office for about thirty minutes when I was summoned to his office. He wanted to know what the two of us were doing in the office until three in the morning. So, I told him. "You published a work plan at the beginning of March which on Friday last called for the tax cards to be prepared. My section sergeant was on leave so it was down to me to see that your order was completed, Sir." He was livid, why didn't we ask for help? I reminded him of his talk he gave earlier in the month. His reply to that was "You are a regular soldier aren't you." "Yes sir" I replied. "The only way I can bust you back to a private is by district court martial, is that right." "Yes sir" I replied. I was dismissed with the warning "Don't do it again."

The only problem now was theses fifteen thousand records had to be signed off by an officer. This entailed each record being stamped with a seal very similar to that used in post offices to day, and initialled by the officer. All six officers had to remain in the afternoon while we went to the beach or where ever. There were always ways for us to get our own back. One was hockey played on the parade ground. The CO was a very keen player, but we made sure that the team we were playing knew who the CO. was. If he got a 'tap' around the ankles, that was just bad luck!

Every year there are three important parades, Queen's birthday, Armistice parade and annual admin inspection. One year I managed to miss all three. For the Queen's birthday parade, I was back in England on leave mid-way through my time in Cyrenaica. The Armistice Parade I was on light duties because I had burnt my left forearm. Between two of the beds was a table that we used to press our uniforms. The guy opposite had put a photo there for me to look at. I leant over the table and leant on the hot iron, putting my whole weight on it. I immediately covered the burn with my body and got a wound dressing out of my locker. I opened it up and slapped it over the burn and bandaged it up and went and reported sick. The medical officer commended me for my prompt action, apparently ninety percent of burns there turned septic due to the dust and sand in the atmosphere. Mine healed with no lasting scar, but not in time for the parade. I also missed the Annual Inspection but I can't remember the reason why.

So, I flew home for a month's leave only to find that my Mum was quite ill but still having to run the shop. I did two things that changed my life. First Mo and I got engaged and the second was I went back to my unit and applied for a compassionate discharge.

It seemed to take an age. On my way home, I spent three days in transit in Malta (where I caught the worst cold in my life) and finally got to the depot situated in the village of Ash to hand my uniform in. It was here that I found out that I should not have used the wound dressing I was issued with. Apparently, it was to be used on the battle field, despite being praised by the doctor and stopping the burn turning septic. I explained this to the soldier who I was handing everything over too and he found one that had been opened and so I didn't have to pay for a replacement. I was finally discharged on the tenth of March 1958, having served just over two years. I guess the delay in getting my discharge was that I had to serve the minimum two-year period of National Service. There was one final restriction. I was notified by the records office that because my clearance was top secret, if ever I wanted to 'go behind the iron curtain' I would have to make a request to the records office for special permission. Because I had been going through all the records that the Pay Office had kept since the end of World War 2 I was classified top secret. The only sensitive knowledge was when the next bullion delivery was arriving at Benina. I can't think that would be very interesting to the Russians, I suppose they could have learnt our strength there by the amount of cash sent out.

To recap, I met Mo when I was fifteen, she was fourteen. I lived in Swindon. She lived in Cardiff. I went into the army, and she was still at school in the upper sixth form. When I left the Army, Mo was at college in Clacton, Essex, training to be a teacher. In all of the seven years we had known each other until the time leading up to getting married we saw each other was just about three times a year. But what we did do was write. I wrote every day and I numbered each letter. In fact, when I sealed one envelope I would number the next one ready for my next episode. Therefore, in my time in the army I must have written about eight hundred letters whereas Mo wrote about five hundred times.

For the next two years I worked for Mum in the shop. Apparently whilst I was overseas the local council bought the field next door to the house for council housing. In the process they found out that should the field ever be sold the owners of Lady's Close had to have first refusal. So, Mum and Dad were offered up to one acre, so they opted for half an acre. It cost fifty pounds. They had a lock up shop built on it with a counter Service grocery shop in the front half and a store room behind. I have to confess, that working in the shop didn't appeal to me. I confess I felt trapped because of my loyalty to Mum.

I enrolled in night school at the college in Swindon on a course leading to an exam set by the Institute of Certified Grocers. Mum signed up to the Spar marketing organisation. This meant we got a wholesaler who sent a representative to take our order each week and we were supplied with posters advertising special offers on discounted lines. The Spar brand originally started in Holland and Mum and I went on a trip to see how it worked. We flew from Heathrow in a WW2 Dakota. The cabin was divided in two by the main wing strut going across the width of the passenger area, which if you were in the forward half involved climbing a couple of steps to access the seats forward of the strut. The result of the trip was that Mum was all fired up with the idea of refitting the shop as a self-service shop. The Spar rep. drew up the plans and we got the local builder to take the stud wall that divided the shop from the store room. Then the shop fitters moved in and fitted the new shelving. As you walked in the left bay window was where the special offers were displayed, and the other window became the check-out area. Also, the outside porch at the rear was bricked in with a window, door and a sink put in. Then some of the shelving units that had been taken out were installed so there was somewhere to put the mugs and tea and coffee stuff. Finally, the coal cellar was turned into the off-licence storeroom. The upstairs had a central full height walking area but the side areas were only five feet, the rest of the wooden shelves were taken up and shortened to fit down both outer walls. Later a lean-too was built to the side of the shop that bordered onto the council houses. This was for pre-packaged coal and coke. It certainly boosted our trade.

Then one day I had an accident with the bacon slicer and managed to slice my finger with the blade as it cut into the fleshy part of my middle finger of my left hand. I knew if mum saw the blood she would feint so I pressed my finger into the palm of my hand and told mum I wouldn't be long. I drove over to the next village to the doctor's surgery. He took one look at it and said, "This is going to hurt." He had been a naval doctor and didn't mess about, he got his needle and the cat gut and put three stitches in. I had to agree, it did hurt.

I continued to go to church, there was a small Methodist chapel in the village. The steward was a Mr Miles. He and his wife had one son and the two of us soon became friends. The minister lived in Farringdon and he opened up his home for the eighteen to twenty five-year olds for bible study and coffee and biscuits once a week. Occasionally we would meet in one of the girl's family home where on one occasion the lads said they would get the supper drinks. We took the orders. One of the girls, Zoe wanted hot chocolate. But we had an alternative on offer. One made with Exlax, but there was a mix up. Instead of Zoe getting the doctored drink, Brian, her boyfriend, ended up with it. At the end of the evening the two started to walk home when Brian announced he would have to run. No further comment! Another bit of mischief was when we doctored a new pack of butter. Half way between the corner of the pack and where the knife we made a slit and there we introduced some Colemans mustard. The pack of butter was carefully re-wrapped and 'Bob's your uncle and Sally's your Aunt.' Job done!

On the outskirts of the village was a WW2 airfield which now was home to a Parachute Battalion. They did a lot of experimental drops which involved dropping fresh eggs from a height of one hundred and fifteen feet in a variety of packaging. The reason was based on the Malaysian war which lasted from 1948 until 1955 and was communist led. If a British or Commonwealth soldier was wounded and needed morphine it had to be dropped into a small clearing in the jungle, the trees of which grew to a height of eighty feet. And of course, a parachute couldn't be used, the chute would get tangled in the tree tops and the wounded soldier wouldn't get his medication. The packaging was eventually perfected.

We struck up a friendship with a couple of the soldiers based there. One, Tait, was a right lad from Northumberland. At the time the Army was using Austin Leyland champ jeeps. Its most unusual fact was that the vehicle could go as fast in reverse as it would in first gear. One-time Tait was driving an officer around the perimeter road. At some point they stopped, and when it was time to set off Tait put the Champ in reverse and accelerated as hard as he could. The officer was soon shouting 'Stop you idiot.' On another occasion he was driving his officer around the camp and, as was his normal self, was messing about. The officer said, 'if you don't stop messing about I'll drive,' Tait immediately started to lift the steering wheel off and both of them were horrified when in fact the wheel rose up and came away from the steering column. The vehicle had just been serviced and the mechanic had failed to replace the nut and safety split pin. Fortunately, the vehicle was safely brought to a stop. But did it put an end of his larking about? No chance! Tait joined our church youth group. When we went out he would sit in the near side back seat with the window open. As we overtook cyclists Tait would lean out of the window shouting 'Ra-ta-ta-ta' and one elderly gentleman fell off his bike.

Dave is a few years older than me. He worked at the local Vauxhall dealership in Faringdon where he was the store's manager; in those days he had to estimate what spare parts he would need for the following month. If something special was required to repair a car the dealer would have to go to Dunstable to collect it. I went with Dave one time after he had finished work. This involved a one hundred-and-twenty-mile round trip to collect the spare part from the gate keeper at the site. Dave had flat feet which meant he was unfit for military service. I realised he may not cope with a battlefield situation, but if he did his national service time it would be served in the U.K. I don't know why he wasn't called up. He was now courting a girl who was a nurse at the Radcliffe hospital in Oxford. Then came the day Dave broke his leg and couldn't drive. He asked me 'Could you drive me to Oxford' with no hesitation I said yes. Off we went, picked up Shelia and then drove to a parking lot by the side of the River Thames, where I got out and went for an hour walk along the river. Fortunately, it was a lovely evening, so I didn't mind. It might have been different if it had been raining. I also drove him to the local hospital when the time came for his plaster to be taken off. His muscles had wasted away so the first step was nearly his last as he stumbled and nearly fell.

By now Mo was living in Clacton on Sea training to be a domestic science teacher, at St. Osyth's College. The number of times we saw each other was strictly limited. My mum would lend me her Morris Minor for the trip. I would start off and drive to London and around the North Circular. Even in the late 1950's it was a nightmare. I found it far easier to drive straight through the city and out through the east end. One of my visits was in the winter and was my first experience of winter in East Anglia. Also Clacton, in winter, did not have many attractions open. One time we tried the doors on all the beach huts on the promenade, and eventually we were lucky and spent a while cuddling up trying to get warm. On another visit we drove out to Flatford Mill, made famous by Constable's painting. On the way back to Clacton we ended up in the ditch. I needed a break down truck to tow us out, and fortunately no damage was done, accept to my pride. My fault for paying Mo to much attention and not enough on the road.

During the college holidays Mo would spend half the time at home in Cardiff and the other half with me in in Watchfield. In the evenings mum and dad would be in the front room while Mo and I would spend the evening in the dining room sharing the only chair near the fireplace. By now Mo was in her third and final year at college, and we were planning our special day. Mo, and her mum and dad of course, did most of the planning, and the plan was to get married in Llandaff Cathedral on 6th August 1960. The hotel was booked for the reception, then the bomb shell arrived. The Queen and the Duke of Edinburgh would be visiting the cathedral on the 6th as well. So, we had to make do with the parish church of All Saints, Llandaff North.

The only part I had to play was how we would get all of my friends and relatives to Cardiff. Dave would be my best man, obviously. He had a full PSV license, so I hired a coach from his employer and he rounded everybody up and drove them down to Cardiff. I travelled down the day before and then in the evening Mo's cousin, Viv, and I drove the car to Newport and left my car there, I didn't want all the graffiti or empty cans put on the car. All my party were safely gathered in the church, Dave and I were there anxiously waiting as well. What I didn't know was my future father-in-law and Mo were driving around and he was saying 'It's not too late to change your mind' Thankfully she didn't. We had the usual wedding photos outside the church, then it was time to run the gauntlet of rice and rose petals being thrown at us.

Eventually we were off to the reception at The Grand Hotel in Westgate Street, right in the centre of Cardiff. We were surprised by how many people were lining the street, then it dawned on us. The Queen and Prince Philip had left the Cathedral and were making their way to Cardiff Docks to board the Royal Yacht Britannia moored in Cardiff docks. They were waving flags and shouting at us and we could only join in with a royal wave. What we didn't realise was our car was the last before the road was closed to all traffic in preparation for the queen's journey. We had our reception with its speeches and toasts and then Mo and I circulated the tables and spoke to as many guests as we could. Then was the time for us to retire and get changed. We went up to the room that had been reserved for us. My mother-in-law told Margaret, Mo's younger sister who was fifteen at the time, to help Mo to change. Without warning she came into the room and I don't know who was more embarrassed, I know I was in my underpants and a shirt. Mo quickly shooed Margaret out in tears. Somebody drove us to the railway station along with quite a few of the guests to see us off. The lady with the broom is my aunt Madge.

The lady with the broom is my Aunt Madge.

Then we were off but only to the next stop, Newport, where we recovered the car and set off on honeymoon for two weeks. We divided our time to a week in the Lake District and a week in Scotland.

Our engagement photo, taken whilst on UK leave.

Mo and her dad, Alf. Hill arriving at the church.

Chapter 4

1960's

We spent the first night in Craven Arms at the Stokesay Inn. As we prepared for bed another shock awaited us. The rose petals that were showered on us at the station had died our clothes and skin, so the first intimate moments were spent scrubbing each other's backs.

In the morning we visited the best preserved fortified medieval Manor House in England, Stokesay Castle. Absolutely enchanting. We continued our journey and toured around the Lake District. We never booked any accommodation in advance, neither of us had gone further afield than North Wales, we wanted to be totally flexible. We visited Lancaster and then on to the Lake District and Lake Windermere, consisting, Esthwaite Water, Ryedale Water, Grasmere and Ullswater, Keswick and Bowness-on Furness. Then it was Hadrian's Wall before driving on to Scotland. We stayed a couple of nights at Gretna Green at the Lovers Leap Motel and of course we went to the Blacksmiths Shop, but we didn't need their services. By this time my camera had crashed so we took to buying post cards of the places we visited. The highlights included Bruce's Cave, in Dumfries, where he watched the spider spinning a web and having to do it over and over again until eventually it did it. We hurried through Glasgow without stopping and onto Lock Lomond and Lock Leven before an overnight stop in Oban and a visit to Glencoe, sight of the Massacre of Glencoe. Thirty-eight men of the MacDonald Clan were killed by government forces billeted with them, on the grounds that they had not pledged their allegiance to the new monarchs, William and Mary. Another forty women and children subsequently died of exposure after their homes were burnt. This took place on the thirteenth of February 1692. Fort William was the start of a visit to the Isle of Sky. We spent a couple of nights on Skye at a crofter's cottage, on the outskirts of Portree. On the advice of the crofter's wife we then went on a tour to the Outer Hebrides. We sailed from Uig to Tarbet and then on to Loch Mandy before returning to Portree for our second night on Skye. We travelled northwards along the shore of Lock Ness and stayed the night at a hotel that was the meeting point for coaches going both north and south and the only accommodation they had were two single rooms. We had no option but to take them. Needless to say, we only used one of the beds.

Once we got to Inverness we started to head south, visiting Braemar, Pitlochry, Sterling ending up in Edinburgh. We stayed at a four-star hotel, The Old Waverley, which at that time was a temperance hotel. We went back to Edinburgh forty years later and had afternoon tea there, which cost more than the two nights bed and breakfast did when we stayed there on our honeymoon.

Before our wedding, both of us decided we didn't want to live with either of our parents. Also, I was tied to helping my mum in the shop, so that limited our options somewhat. We decided on a mobile home which had been sighted and connected up to the various services while we were away. We were able to start our married life on our own. The mobile home was thirty-one feet long by ten feet wide and had a double bedroom and a single bedroom with bunk beds. A kitchen, a bathroom and a lounge diner and it came fully furnished. In the picture one looks into the kitchen and you see the bathroom window. It cost nine hundred and ninety pounds which I had managed to save from my army days. Later on, my father-in-law built us a porch to give us a bit of extra space. We were very happy there. The only thing missing was a small fridge, so I cut into the wall of the bunk bedroom and placed a small fridge on the bunk base. Perfect!

All to soon September was upon us and Mo had secured a teaching post at Jenning Street secondary modern school in Swindon. This meant a couple of bus rides into Swindon each day. She had trained to be a home economics teacher, which included cooking and needlework. As you can imagine she was petrified, and so we began by practicing at home, she would teach me to cook the meal she would teach at school the next day. A few months later I would make and ice the Christmas cake. Also, when we realised Mo was pregnant she taught me to knit. I knitted a white matinee coat, which when it was finished turned out to be slightly grey. But the experience would stand me in good stead in the coming years.

Our mobile home.

Happy days and the start of a life time together.

Our first daughter, Julia, was born on the sixteenth of November nineteen sixty-one, after a very difficult pregnancy. Mo's water broke at twenty-six weeks and she was admitted into our local hospital in Stratton for bed rest when suddenly she went into labour. An ambulance was summoned and with blue lights and sirens blaring she was rushed to the maternity hospital in Old Town, Swindon, only to request a bedpan. With taking things very carefully Julia sat tight and went to full term. Was that possible? Or was it a miracle? *Miracle* Then the next problem was Mo's blood group was O-negative, which apparently was not compatible with mine and might result in any subsequent babies being 'blues babies' and that would mean having a complete blood transfusion. On hearing this we both prayed that this would not be necessary. Our next miracle which the Lord was to answer would be all of our subsequent children didn't need a blood transfer, Praise the Lord. *Miracle*

But then my mum stepped in. "You can't possibly bring up the little one in a caravan. We'll swap! You have the house and Dad and I will move into the caravan." Done, settled, no arguments, we could do nothing but agree. Julia was about six weeks old and I wanted to celebrate the arrival of our daughter by taking Mo out for an evening meal. I arranged for a baby sitter to come into the house, so Mo agreed. At the appointed time he arrived. Yes, he was a boy. Mo was horrified, how could a teenage boy be trusted with our daughter. I had to explain his father was the regimental sergeant major and the whole family were Catholics. The home was run on military lines and each person had their allotted tasks and responsibilities. The mother looked after the baby for the first year and then the two eldest children, our baby sitter and his younger sister took on the responsibility of looking after the youngest member of the family. On the understanding that the lad had the phone number of the restaurant and that we could be back home in ten minutes Mo eventually agreed to go. We had a nice meal, although I knew Mo was a bit apprehensive even though there was no phone call, so as soon as we had finished I paid the bill and we made our way home. What did we find? Julia had woken up and was in the lad's arms with a dirty nappy on the floor and Julia finishing off the second half of the bottle. Mo was astounded, and the lad became our regular baby sitter. I gave him a pound and the next day he came into the shop. He bought some sweets for himself and then stood and thought. 'I wonder what I can get Mum, I know, she was getting low of soap powder, I'll get her a new box.' Apparently, the children's earnings had to be divided. A quarter to their saving account, they could spend a quarter, the next quarter was put aside for replacement clothes and the final quarter to get something for mother.

I got carried away there about our evening out, incidentally I bought Mo a real fur coat as a thank you gift. We were just the same as hundreds of other parents with their child's first year, and I could fill this book with photos of her progress. One time I laid down on the half landing and took a photo when Julia was about eight months old trying to climb the stairs. It was like climbing a mountain. We realised she would soon master the climb but coming down would be different. One of us would carry her up to the half landing and put her down and gently pull her down feet first. As she started to climb again we would pull her down feet first, and within a couple of days she had mastered the technique and we never did buy a stair gate.

But back to the house. When you live in a small place you think tidy, and everything has its place. So, we started moving our things across to the house next door. We had got about half of it in when we ran out of space!

This photo shows the master bedroom with the bay window, behind it is the second double bedroom. Underneath the master bedroom is the lounge which goes from the front to back of the house and has French doors leading into the conservatory. The landing window can be just seen on the right. The landing was so big we had a single bed which came in quite useful when we had guests staying. The whole plot was about half an acre. It was good that dad really enjoyed gardening, because I didn't.

At the end of the first year of teaching Mo and I drove down to Cardiff and left Julia with her grandparents, while we went for a week touring Wales. We first made our way to the Gower peninsular, one of Mo's favourite spots where her family spent most of their summer holidays during and after the war. Then we made our way up the coast of Cardigan Bay and then to North Wales. We drove over to Anglesey and we had to visit the famous station. At that time, you had to purchase a penny ticket to go on a platform, but here it cost two pence because the ticket was twice as long.

'Llanfairpwllgwyngyllgogerychwyrndrobwllllantysiliogogogoch.'

It took Mo the rest of the week to teach me to say it and I still remember it to this day. We took the train to the top of Snowdon and walked down. Truly a very memorable week.

Our second chilled, Teresa was born on the twenty eighth of April, 1963. Mo's waters broke whilst she was in the bath and she hadn't realised it. The baby was not hanging around and so I had to help Mo out of the bath and carry her into the bedroom and place her on the bed. Then I phoned the midwife who arrived just in time for a home delivery. There was no time to consider if the baby would need a complete blood transfusion. It was then that The Lord had answered our prayer about blue babies.

I was there fetching and carrying and at some point, I went back to the shop so Mum could pop over to the house to satisfy herself everything was alright. On her way out, Mum inadvertently closed the door so hard and the door handle fell on to the floor on the landing outside. Fortunately, Mo and the baby were in the single bedroom which overlooks the front, so Mo had to wait for a pedestrian to walk past the front gate. Fortunately, Mo didn't have to wait long and was successful in getting one of the local ladies to come in and remedy the situation.

Our trip to the Isle of White.

Early in June nineteen sixty-three we went on a short holiday with Julia and our second child, Teresa who was a five-week-old. Also, my sister-in-law, Margaret, and her boyfriend Peter came too. We drove down to Portsmouth and caught the ferry over to the Isle of Wight where we camped. Because it was the May half term holiday, when we came to book the return ferry the only one which had any space was the last ferry on the Friday evening to Lymington. We arrived there at about ten o'clock in the evening and pitched our tents somewhere in the new forest in the pouring rain. We all huddled together in one of the tents and put the kettle onto boil for a hot drink before hitting the hay. Half way through the boil the camping Gaz cylinder ran out of butane. I dashed out to get a replacement cylinder and, in my haste, only clipped two of the three lugs, the gas was escaping and as soon as I entered the tent the gas went up to the pressure lantern hanging from the ridge of the tent. I was left holding the flaming cylinder which was more like a flaming blow torch. I quickly realised I had two options, either to hold the flame away from me, but that meant directing the flame on everyone else including Mo who was holding Teresa in her arms. I really only had the alternative option open to me, I turned the flame onto myself. Fortunately, the tent door was still open, so I turned and threw the flaming torch outside, but in my haste didn't throw it far enough. I picked it up and threw it further away and then rolled over in the grass to put the flames out that were on me.

Peter rushed out and wrapped a blanket round me and then he and Mo drove me around the new forest until we found a telephone box. We dialled 999 and waited for an ambulance which arrived quite quickly and took me and Mo into Lymington Cottage hospital, while Peter went back to where we had pitched the tents. They had to leave the next day, Saturday, because Teresa was being christened in the local Methodist chapel on the Sunday. Peter and Meg were to be stand in parents and also God parents.

Meanwhile Mo had found a bed and breakfast in the village. She woke up to the smell of smoke, she found that her hair, which was tied in a ponytail, now consisted of a rubber band and just a few strands of hair. The rest had been burnt away. In the meantime, my burns were assessed as second-degree facial burns and third-degree arms burns from the knuckles to where the arms of my t-shirt came to on both arms. These had been dressed in a Vaseline impregnated gauze and then covered with a roll of cotton wool and then bandaged. Within twenty minutes I was dripping body fluids and liquid Vaseline. Early on the Monday morning a male staff nurse came and examined my arms. He redressed them and then sat on the edge of the bed and explained what would happen next. The hospital was GP led and he predicted that the GP would recommend that I be transferred immediately to Salisbury hospital which had a special burns unit. The nurse went on to tell me that during WW2 he had been a medical orderly in the R.A.F. patching up wounded air crew returning from bombing raids over Germany. He suggested to me that I should tell the GP that I wanted to think about it. That was exactly what happened. I realised that the nurse had more experience in treating burns than the GP, so I decided to take the nurses' advice. Because I wanted to defer my decision, the GP washed his hands of me and I never saw him again. However, I do thank God for that nurse who told me to wait. I just knew that that was what I had to do, I had to put my faith in the Lord and not doubt. It took time. I was still having my dressings applied and the only thing I could wear was a hospital gown. The muscles in my arms had contracted and I had very little movement of my lower arms, so I walked around the ward like a zombie. Meal times were quite difficult, I could get the food on a dessert spoon and lift it up towards my mouth but couldn't bend my arm sufficiently for me to get the spoon to my mouth. The solution was to turn by head and look at my shoulder, then with my fingers gripping the spoon ninety degrees and then popping the spoon into my mouth as it passed by, so to speak. As I said, meals times were quite difficult, but to anybody watching, it was quite hilarious. Lymington hospital was a cottage hospital with just two wards - male and female. And the majority of men were elderly and suffering from heart complaints. By Tuesday I had determined that if I wanted to get better I would have to get on with life, so when the wash trolley came around in the morning, I was there helping to push the trolley to the bed sides. I couldn't use my arms so I used my stomach, with the philosophy "where there's a will, there is a solution." One elderly gentleman called me aside and said I was a tremendous encouragement to him as in his opinion, I was in a much more serious condition than he was.

I was there about ten days before I was discharged and Mo drove me home to Watchfield. By now fresh skin was growing under the burnt layer and I was beginning to peal. Itch! I had never experienced irritation like it, it had to come off! I would pull off strips of skin four or five inches in length, and the next layer would grow and then die and have to be pulled off. Eventually after a few weeks I stopped pealing and first my face and then my arms returned to normal without any disfigurement or scaring. If I had listened to the doctor I would have had skin grafts and the subsequent scars. *Miracle*

In the mean time we had a holiday booked for a cabin cruiser on the Norfolk Broads. Mo was knitting herself a sweater in preparation for the chilly evenings on the boat. I said I wanted one too. She gave me needles and pattern and got more wool out of the shop. And so, I started knitting the only problem was I am a very tight knitter, so I had to knit a larger size, but I finished it before the holiday and it fitted. My recuperation was complete. The holiday had been booked way back and we were a group of friends, enough to hire two twelve birth boats and we filled every birth. We organised the crew, so that those with families would always lead the convoy. I was skipper on the first boat, David, who had been with me on one holiday on the Norfolk Broads before, was skipper on the following boat. The first time he took control was on one of the rivers and he had just turned into a cutting to enter one of the Broads. The boat had a forward steering position just like a car, you sat in an armchair and had a steering wheel in front of you. I was at the back of the boat when he shouted to me "Where's the brake!" Being in the motor trade he was used to cars, but this was his first time afloat. I was able to take control of the situation and we avoided the sailing boat coming the other way.

My logic was that if one of the children accidentally fell overboard they would be ok because they all wore their life jackets all the time. But it would be quicker for the second boat to pick up the child than the first could because they would have to turn my boat around. We practiced the procedure by throwing a washing bowl over the side which was successfully picked up and handed to us when David steered alongside. It was a hilarious time as we fooled around. While we were in one of the Broads we got the washing up liquid containers and tried to hit someone on the other boat. That game ended abruptly when our boat hit the other boat in the side of the forward cabin just above one of the bunks with our stern quarter. We declared it when we got back to the boat yard; the boat was covered by the insurance. On another time all of us stood on the cabin roof to have our photo taken. Instead of telling us all to move back, Cliff, who was taking the photo, did and we didn't warn him he was about to topple backwards into the water, which he did!

Family life was perfect. We had two wonderful girls and supportive parents. Mo had completed her year of probation as a teacher but was now enjoying being a full-time mum with lots of friends. The closest were John and Eunice who lived in Stratton and went to the same church as David and Sheila. Mo also had good friend living in the village. There were picnics in Savernake Forest and in the grounds of the Royal Military College of Science just a mile down the road. It was here that Julia took her first steps on the lawn outside the officers' mess. When Teresa was about eighteen months old I went upstairs for something and as I looked out of the landing window at the fir tree, growing just outside the window, there to my surprise was Teresa climbing up the tree. She was only eighteen months old, heaven forbid! I rushed down and out the front door and there was Julia egging Teresa on, 'You can do it.' This was characteristic of both girls, Teresa was the first to get into any trouble that was going because she was an independent strong character. Julia on the other hand was always more the instigator, she would not point at anything but grab the nearest finger and point. She had been told that it was rude to point. But it was like firing a gun, Julia would load the revolver and get Teresa to point the gun, but it was Julia's finger that pulled the trigger so to speak.

Because we lived so near to my parents and Mo's lived in Cardiff we made a point of spending Christmas with them. We would drive down on Christmas Eve; the first few times we had to drive up to Gloucester and then thru Chepstow and then through Newport to get to 77 Station Rd. Llandaff North. A couple of years later part of the M4 had opened, but over the Christmas period it had snowed quite hard and the motorway was down to one lane only. I and the rest of the traffic were following a Mini car which suddenly started to go slower and slower until it stopped completely. All four wheels had left the ground and the floor of the car was resting on the snow Several drivers got out and pushed the car onto the hard shoulder and unsympathetically left him there. The next year we decided to go by train. We parked the car in the car park of the Railway Inn outside Swindon station. As usual it snowed over the holiday period but when we got back to the car we couldn't find it. We had parked the car at the side of an outbuilding and the snow on the roof had slid down and virtually buried the car. I scraped the snow off the bonnet and checked that no snow had got into the distributor and started the car first time. We drove home with about two feet of snow on the roof of the car. It then took me a couple of hours to clear the drive sufficiently to be able to get the car in off the road.

During the summer holidays of nineteen sixty-four we had a holiday at Butlins in Bognor Regis. We were attracted to it as an ideal venue for families with young children. There were good childminding services and their catering facilities were excellent. However, it didn't quite work out as we planned. Mo and I contracted food poisoning and so we cut short our holiday and drove home.

In Nineteen sixty-five The Sound of Music was released and we went to see it. Mo fell in love with it and I decided to surprise her. I arranged for Shelia and David to have the children for a week and we flew to Salzburg where we hired a Volkswagen Beetle. We went to the mansion used in the film set and the convent and the castle. Mo was in her element. But we also explored the city of Salzburg and took a ride in a horse drawn carriage. And of course, you cannot go so Salzburg with experiencing the music of Mozart.

We visited a bishop's palace in nearby Hellbrun. It was built in 1613–19 by Markus Sittikus von Hohenems, Prince-Archbishop of Salzburg, and named for the "clear spring" that supplied it. Hellbrun was only meant for use as a day residence in summer. The Schloss is famous for its water games conceived by Markus Sittikus, a man with a keen sense of humour, as a series of practical jokes to be performed on guests. Notable features include stone seats around a stone dining table through which a water conduit sprays water into the seat of the guests when the mechanism is activated, and hidden fountains that surprise and spray guests while they take part sitting at the table. Other features are a mechanical, water-operated and music playing theatre built in 1750 including some 200 displays showing various professions at work, a grotto and a crown being pushed up and down by a jet of water, symbolising the rise and fall of power. At all of these games there is always a spot which is never wet, that is where the Archbishop stood or sat, to which there is no water conduit and which is today where the guide stands.

It must have been in nineteen sixty-four that Julia began to experience stomach pains. We took her to see the village doctor, and he explained to us that sometimes infections were manifested as a throat infection, other times they would go to the stomach. She was given a course of antibiotics and it seemed to work. But over the next two years this was a reoccurring problem and there were frequent visits to the doctor and courses of antibiotics.

We travelled down to Cardiff for the May bank holiday in nineteen sixty-seven, Mo's sister, Margaret (Meg to everyone) was getting married on the bank holiday Saturday. Their brother Clive had come over from Montreal, Canada for the event and he travelled back with us on the Monday. The journey was horrendous, not only was the traffic bad but Julia screamed the whole way. We gave her some pain killers which did ease the pain.

The next day we were driving Clive back to Heathrow for his flight back to Canada, but we made an urgent appointment to see our GP. His advice was that we should take Julia into the hospital in Swindon just for observation. She was admitted, and Mo decided to continue on to Heathrow as nothing would happen to Julia as she was being 'observed.' When we got to Heathrow, we phoned the hospital and was horrified when we were told that Julia had had her operation.

We said our good byes to Clive and headed back to Swindon where we met one of the doctors who attended the operation. He showed us a piece of metal about five centimetres in length. Both ends were sharp as needles and we were told that they had operated because they suspected the appendix might be the root of the problem. However, that organ was normal, but the intestine wall was inflamed and that led to the discovery of the piece of metal imbedded in the wall of the intestine and removed it. He asked if we knew what it was and I immediately said, "where is the other half." I recognised it as a woman's hair grip because for a third of its length it was convoluted.

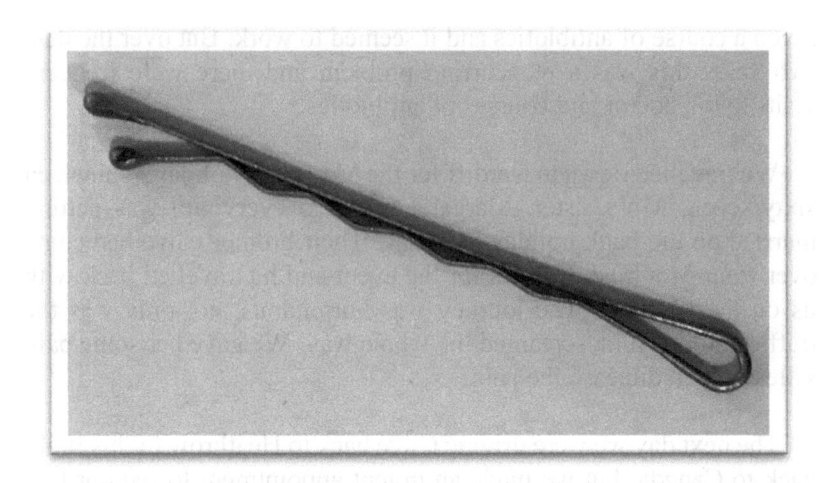

Obviously, it had been in Julia's stomach for so long the plastic 'cushions' on the two ends had disappeared and now there were two pieces with four needle sharp ends. He said that this one piece was all that had been removed but acting on this new information five days later Julia was subjected to a Barium Meal X-ray which showed the other half still in the stomach. Apparently, her inside was just like a sieve where food travelling around came across the hairpin, that was too large to get around the twists and turns of the stomach and was being pushed out of that part of the stomach which is when Julia would scream her head off. A second major operation would be needed to remove it. I had to acknowledge that all the penicillin Julia had taken over the previous two or more years might have helped in keeping the risk of infection at bay, but if either of these objects punctured a major blood vessel then the penicillin would not have saved her life. We both realised that God had been looking after her for all this time. *Miracle*

But this was not the end of the affair. Because Julia had under gone two major operations and the barium meal X-ray in ten days the shock to her system meant she was now diagnosed with Petite Mal and she then had to take special medicines to control this, which is a form of Epilepsy. We were told that there was a chance that she would grow out of it or we might find that she would develop into a full Epileptic sufferer. We would know when she was seven years old.

In the intervening two and a half years, I realised that I would have to commit my life to my Saviour, the Lord Jesus. It took me two years and during lent in nineteen sixty-eight the Methodists in the village joined with the Anglicans and one week the meeting was held in the front room of our house. I sat in the dining room and after the meeting the vicar asked me where I stood, to which I replied that I felt as if I was half a Christian. He told me quite categorically that that was impossible, I was either in or out. To which I replied that that was how I felt. We agreed to leave it like that but if I found out the answer I would tell him. A week later I was Baptised by total immersion and was also Baptised in the Spirit. I did go back to the vicar and told him of my experience. Sadly, he pooh-poohed the idea. Then I had a dream that the Lord had healed our daughter and that we should stop the medication. I shared this with Mo and we both agreed we should both go and see our local doctor, who was also a very committed Christian of the Anglian Church. He said "As a doctor I must strongly caution you against this but as a Christian if you believe the Lord has told you to stop, then you should obey Him." We did, and a couple of months later we had an appointment to see an RAF doctor who gave Julia a most thorough examination. After he had finished he told us that no longer did Julia suffer from the Petite Mal and we could discontinue the medication. Then I confessed that Jesus had told us that three months ago to do just that. He couldn't say a word! *Miracle*

We were thrilled to have a son. This highlighted the reason I was christened 'Philip Nowell.' Mum was very clear that she was proud and wanted the family name of 'Nowell' to continue. She was one of nine children, five of which were boys and therefore four were girls. However, two of the boys, Charles and Thomas died in infancy. This left three boys, Harry, Horace and Len to continue the Nowell family name. It started off well, Harry had two sons, John and Jeremy. Horace had two daughters, Anne and Sara and Len had one daughter, Pauline. Mum's fear that the name would die out hence my Christian name being registered 'Philip Nowell' through ignorance. I realised that she did her best and the birth of our son Ian brought this into focus. He was born on the tenth of November 1965. I decided to change my surname to 'Nowell-Smith' by Deed Poll which I signed on the thirty first of December nineteen sixty-five. John Nowell had one daughter and at present I know Jeremy married but died young, leaving behind two sons.

When Ian was just two years old we took a short break to Holland. It was supposed to be a surprise for Mo, but she wanted our bedroom fitted out with new wardrobes, I said I couldn't afford it. She knew what was in the bank and that we could afford to have a revamp of our bedroom. So, I had to come clean and say I had booked a surprise holiday to Holland. She didn't believe my saying we can't go, the children don't have passports. I had to show her my passport with the three children added so that she would believe me. When I announced that we were going the following weekend, apparently that meant that we had to start getting everything together, and you know what that means, clothes sorted, and Mo had to have her hair done. I had decided that we would take our car as with the three children it would be more convenient. On arrival in Holland we drove to The Hague and found a lovely motel. Apart from the bathroom, the remaining room was all open plan with two sleeping quarters enclosed by curtains and then with a kitchen area and dining area. I really wanted to visit the model at the Madurodam. Mo was looking forward to visiting the Keukenhof. Then there were the canals and the various waterways. The children, including me, were fascinated as we went around the Madurodam; in addition to the double O railway there were cars and lorries moving along the roads, aircraft taxiing around the airport and ships negotiating the harbour. The detailing was so precise. Mo was equally impressed with the displays at the Keukenhof, which is a permanent display of Dutch flower growers showing off their wares. Mo brought back some tulip bulbs for the garden. We went on a boat tour around the harbour and the canals. And the children, especially Julia, enjoyed themselves especially running around the flower beds at the Keukenhof.

By the time that Julia had been healed from her petite Mal, Ian was learning to ride his handed-down two-wheel bike with stabilisers on the rear wheels. He had got the hang of it and could balance well and without losing his balance. However, he hadn't mastered the brakes to stop. We were watching him cycling across the lawn toward the huge leylandii hedge that had encroached onto the lawn. Ian disappeared from view. We got him out covered in the leaves of the leylandii, thankfully no damage except to his pride. It wasn't long before he started school at the local infant school, where I was now a school governor.

It was about this time that Teresa had a disagreement with her Mother and she was going to 'run away to the spare garage. It couldn't be used as the nearby trees had cracked and lifted the floor in several places, and thus the double door could not be shut properly. In addition, there was no electricity laid on and there were spiders and their webs everywhere.

Mum was busy as well. Julia and Ian decided to join Teresa. We had kept the baby listening gadget and we installed it, so we could be aware of any trouble that occurred. It was quite amusing as the children constantly journeyed back and forth as they realised more things they would need. Bedding, drinks, sandwiches and torches.

Mo settled Julia and Ian into bed and made sure they were comfortable, but Teresa refused all help. Then we settled down in the house to listen to their chatter. It gradually died down as one by one they fell asleep. They had a better night's sleep than we did as we took turns to 'listen in.'

In the morning they came in and took out bowls of cornflakes for their breakfast. They couldn't work out how breakfast was ready for us, with the cereal that was decided upon on the evening before. Little did they know that we were listening into these conversations.

We persuaded Julia to come indoors the next evening because of her asthma. Ian lasted another night before he was also brought back. Next day Teresa, after one night alone, also gave up her protest and peace and harmony was restored.

Ian, Julia and Teresa, with the garage they 'ran away' to.

In nineteen sixty-seven the Lord impressed on both Mo and I that we should open our home to the old folk of the village on Christmas Day, who would otherwise be alone. At the time we were meeting with another couple who lived in Army married quarters. He was a chef in the catering corps. Both Malcolm and Doris were very committed Christians, so we shared our vision with them. All four or us reached out in prayer for the number we would have to cater for. We all agreed on the figure thirty. It was easy to get the word out. We just had the one postman who lived in the village and he regularly delivered the mail. I printed the invites and he delivered them to those who would spend Christmas alone. Christmas Day arrived and eighteen turned up for dinner and then eleven came to tea. They all had a wonderful time and it was the subject of conservation for weeks to come. We were perplexed however as we sure the Lord had said thirty, but only twenty-nine turned up. Then we realised one lady had come to lunch and stayed for tea. The Lord had the perfect number. *Miracle*

Throughout this whole period from nineteen sixty-seven until nineteen seventy-one we were attending a house church in Swindon, led by Mike Ranstead, with about twenty people there each week. Every so often we had a visiting speaker come including the pastor of South Chard Church, Sid Purse. On one of these visits Mo and I were both baptised in the Ranstead's bath by Uncle Sid and Mike. Then when we went back downstairs all the fellowship gathered around us and laid hand on us and they prayed that we would be baptised in the Spirit and speak in 'Tongues.' Other visiting speakers from the church at South Chard included Harry Greenwood, Tony Nash, Ian Andrews, Andrew Jordan and Ralph St John. There are many books written about the Church at South Chard over the years including one by Margaret Joy which told the story of how the church came into being. Harry Greenwood wrote a series of short addresses which has now been published as 'Light in your darkness' and Margaret Hall entitled 'What a Coincidence' which tells how she and her husband came to move to Chard and join the Fellowship.

By this time Mum and Dad had traded in the caravan they were living in and bought a mobile home which they sited in the garden of the house, right at the back corner of the garden. This enabled me to open up a petrol filling station on the site. I bought a lock up garage to serve as the office. We chose to go with Jet petrol, the cut price arm of Conoco. The opening price was four gallons for nineteen shillings and eleven pence; a penny short of pound. In nineteen sixty-seven Mum and Dad went into partnership with her youngest brother, Len, and his wife Margaret. They had their mobile home loaded onto a couple of low loaders and re-sighted it at Burnham on Sea. We were also in the process of erecting a workshop to repair cars when disaster struck.

I had negotiated a loan from the bank when Harold Wilson's Government announced a credit squeeze. What was I to do, the actual workshop was up but there was still equipment to buy. Was I to abandon the project? I decided to try and keep going. Suppliers to both shop and garage were forced to wait longer until they were paid.

Then on New Year's Day nineteen seventy The Lord told me what I should do. I woke up with the word "Liquidate." I phoned my accountant and later that day I went into his office and we talked through how and what would happen. Most importantly I was not to give any favour to one supplier over another. It was agreed that the businesses should be kept going until at least until the creditors agreed to what should be done.

Finally, I was no longer able to order supplies directly. All requests for supplies had to be signed by the administrator. So sometime in March the creditors met and it was decided to try and sell the two businesses and our home as a going concern as one lot. Also, I was asked if I would stay on as manager until all was sold. And to do this they would pay me a salary, which was more that I had been drawing from the business during the last twelve months.

I had been quite proud of my achievements in the village. I have already mentioned that I was a school governor, but I was also a parish councillor and I was instrumental in getting street lighting into the village and a bus shelter erected on the main road. The chairman of the parish council had held that office for many years, it was assumed by everyone he would be the chairman for years to come. I lobbied that the vice chairman would be elevated to chairman after three years and also the chairman could serve for a maximum of six years before having to stand down. This was eventually passed, so now I had become the vice chairman. So, I thought I had good reason to be proud of my achievements, I was a successful businessman, I was a member of the local golf club and well respected in the village. Now my pride had been stripped away. If any supplier was to give me credit the order had to be countersigned by the liquidator, if any of my customers wanted credit I had to refuse and then explain why I had to refuse. But eventually a buyer was found and the date of completion was set for the fourteenth of February nineteen seventy-one.

Chapter 5

We Move to Somerset

We decided that we would spend a weekend in South Chard and arranged to stay at the Manor House which was the home of Uncle Sid and Auntie Mill. We managed to rent a farm house situated just off the A30 road near Cricket St Thomas in the hamlet of Lydmarsh. It had four bedrooms, lounge, dining room and a kitchen. Mo asked if we could rent it from the week before Christmas nineteen seventy and that was agreed. Mo wanted to get the three children settled in to their new school at the beginning of the spring term in January. So, we moved in on Saturday the nineteenth of December nineteen hundred and seventy. Ruth was just three months old. We didn't realise at the time, but she would spend her first birthday in her seventh home.

The fourteenth of February soon came around. During the six weeks of January and February I had been commuting down to Somerset on the Saturday evening and driving back on Tuesday morning. For years, in fact ever since we were married, I had been trying to give up smoking. I had started as a teenager using the money mum had given me to go to Saturday morning cinema, but with a mate we would buy ten Woodbines and go into the church cemetery of St Mark's, the back wall of which would look over to the railway works and the main Bristol to Paddington railway line. We would stand on the stone wall and look over the fence and smoke our cigarettes. I had made a promise to Mo that when I moved to Somerset I would stop smoking. Needless to say, I had made these promises before and even vowed to only smoke outside the house which did help to reduce the number of cigarettes I smoked. Then a friend in the fellowship at Swindon challenged me by saying 'we all know you smoke, so who are you trying to deceive by going outside to smoke.' I wasn't trying to deceive anyone, it was just a tool to reduce the number of cigarettes I smoked in a day, which by this time was about thirty a day. I arrived at the farm house on the thirteenth of February with the worst cold I had ever had in my life. I retired to bed for the next three days and sweated the cold out. I have never smoked or even wanted a cigarette from that day to this. In fact, I give the Lord the credit for my deliverance. In four days I couldn't even bare the smell to tobacco on peoples' clothes, something I had never smelled before. *Miracle*

When we finally left Watchfield we had lost everything, our home, our livelihood, our car, and our friends. Our original plan was to emigrate to Canada. Clive and Leslie had offered to put us up, we could move into the basement of their home in Montreal. When Clive bought a new car, he kept the old one for me. The plan was that we would go into partnership and buy a motel. We had even gone to the office of the Canadian High Commission for our medical examination. We were told that we would have to wait for the decision. If we enquired the enquiry would be ignored. The months went by and perhaps eighteen months or more had gone by when we were forced to move. We both accepted the fact that the Lord had put a stop to that particular dream, so we settled on South Chard in order to follow the Lord more closely. Having since been to Canada, and discovering just what a wonderful place it would be to bring up our family, I would have gone up to London and banged on the door of the High Commission's office. As it has turned out we are still waiting to hear the result of our medicals after fifty years or so. I used to speculate as to how the years would have turned out, none of the children would have married those who they eventually did, or taken the paths that they have. It would have been a different life.

But that was a waste of time, the fact was that I needed a job. I presented myself to the labour office. They didn't have a job for me and because the country was in the grip of a postal strike they were unable to check my entitlement to unemployment benefits; all that I was to be given was an emergency advance of ten pounds a week. This was exactly what we were paying for the farm house. The ten pounds did include the coal for the Aga and as much 'raw' milk as we liked from the bulk tank in the dairy.

David bought an older model Vauxhall Victor estate car which he gave to me. We were allowed to bring our personal belongings with us and there was a spare room in the farm house where we were living.

It was on the upper floor and the door was infested with wood worm, you could vertically see through the door. As we put our furniture in we prayed the Lord would protect it. We had to leave just before the Easter holiday, but we were allowed to leave the furniture there without charge for just over a year. When we did collect it not one piece had been attacked by woodwork. *Miracle*

We would collect the milk and put it in a large saucepan and par boil it on the Aga. Gradually a thick crust of cream would form and then it was left overnight standing on a marble shelf at the end of the rear passage way. We had lots of visitors who came to see us most days and we encouraged them to bring an empty jam jar because we were collecting so much cream.

The children started school at the start of term. It was a long day especially for Ian. They had to walk up the hill to the main road from Crewkerne to Chard where they were picked up by the school mini bus. Ian especially enjoyed living on a farm. There was plenty of things to keep him happy, chasing the hens around the yard and going with the farmer to bring the cows in for milking. He would quite often go into the pig field at the back of the house. There was a latch gate from the garden directly into the field. One day his feet sank into the wet mud and fell head first into the mess. He had to stand in the gateway while mum hosed him down before he was stripped off and put in the bath.

I had only been in the farm house for a couple of weeks when I was asked if I would like to go to Israel for an eight-day tour. It would change my life. I soaked up all the places in Jerusalem we visited, I also visited the Dead Sea and Masada and Galilee. I came back with a deep love for Israel and the Jewish people. To my surprise Vince Matherick, who ran a business called Fellowship Tours from his home in one of the bungalows in South Chard, asked me if I would be prepared to lead a tour. He had assembled people who had seen his adverts in the various Christian press. The group consisted of just over forty people. I think the opportunity of visiting Israel decided it for me. At the time I didn't give much thought about the responsibilities I would have to take on. For me the crunch time came when we reached Tiberius. We had been visiting the biblical sites around the shores of the Lake - Capernahum, Tabgha, where we remembered the feeding of the five thousand, and the small chapel of St. Peter Primacy, where Jesus asked Peter 'Do you love me, feed my sheep.' After dinner we had agreed to meet, and I would lead the meeting. I had never done anything like this ever before. I made my way up onto the flat roof of the Church of Scotland Hospice, where we were staying where I could guarantee I would be alone. I prayed to the lord to guide me, to put His words into my mouth, and to fill me with His Holy Spirit. Then it was time to re-join the group. It all went fine. From those two visits a lifelong love of Israel and its people, both Jew and Arab have led to lifelong friendships. As this story progresses no doubt I'll return to events in Israel.

Because I was 'on the dole' I made myself available to help the farmer. At the time he was converting a building that had been used to house chickens to be used as a piggery, so I found myself creating pig sties' out of breeze blocks. That was a new experience! I went to the midweek service one Wednesday evening. Before the service I went into the Manor House where I was asked by a man there what I had been doing that day. I replied truthfully 'building pigsties' to which he replied quite seriously 'unclean, unclean' to which I replied 'if a man wants to eat he should work for it' needless to say it was all harmless banter.

Easter had come and it was time to leave the farm house, and so started a period of time when we moved quite frequently. We were able to rent a holiday let at another farm at the 'drift' very near to Lydmarsh for two weeks. After this we moved to Green End farm until the May bank holiday when it had already been let out to another family. Again, I made myself available, this time helping with the silage. Bill, the farmer, would bring the silage into the yard and tip it out. My job was to drive the 'Fergie' tractor which was fitted with a rake at the back. I would reverse into the grass then reverse it up the grass ramp, when the whole load had been moved I would drive the tractor up and down compressing the grass in order that it would become silage. This was the first time I had driven a tractor and it was years later that I found out that what I had been doing was the most dangerous job on a farm. Many farm workers were injured and even killed when a tractor tipped over with the farm worker pinned underneath it. Obviously, the Lord was looking after me. *Miracle*

Ian again would go with the farmer to bring the cows in for milking. He became very useful in helping to move the electric fence. Bill didn't like the jolt the fence gave you if you touched it. If it was 'live' Ian wasn't at all effected by it. There was one cow in the herd that had a horrible limp and Ian and Teresa prayed for her every day until she was healed. One day we were all sat around the dining table for lunch. As was my practice I asked the children to close their eyes as I prayed that the Lord would bless the food we were about to eat. What they didn't know was there was no food in the house to eat. But we are reminded in Matthew 21:22 And Jesus answered them, "Truly, I say to you, if you have faith and do not doubt, you will not only do what has been done to the fig tree, but even if you say to this mountain, be taken up and thrown into the sea,' it will happen. And whatever you ask in prayer, you will receive, if you have faith." Ian must have prayed with his eyes open because as I said 'Amen' he said, "Who is that that just walked pass the window." Nobody ever came to the front door. Everyone came to the back yard. I went to the front door and I could see about two hundred yards up the road in front of the house and about the same distance to the right. There wasn't a soul in sight, but there was a box of food. Dinner had arrived and not only dinner but enough food for the rest of the week. Yet another miracle! *Miracle* In the same way that the children were taught how to do things, like how to go down the stairs safely even though they couldn't walk and after a few times they knew how to and do it automatically, so they needed to learn how to have to have faith in God's provision.

We had to vacate Green End because their bookings were coming in fast and furious. Even Auntie Mill was full for the May bank holiday but after the weekend we could move into her caravan that was parked behind the church. So, we arranged to drive back to

Swindon and stay with Mike Ranstead and his family. During the week preceding the bank holiday we had be given a number of cash gifts. When I counted them up it amounted to just over seventy pounds. I hadn't had that much money in my hand since living in Wiltshire. Why did we need all this money? We set off on the Friday morning and when we got to Swindon I realised the car exhaust was blowing. Now I knew why the Lord had obviously impressed on various Christians to give us what we would need. On the Saturday the car was repaired and we had just enough money to pay for it. *Miracle* It seems to me as I write my story that miracles are happening thick and fast in my life!

On the Tuesday we drove back to South Chard, it rained for the whole journey. The rain fell in buckets. We had the three children in the back seat, Mo held Ruth in her arms, the cot mattress and bedding were in the boot but the framework for the cot was strapped down on the roof rack. It was a terrible journey, and a slow one because of the poor visibility. But eventually we arrived and parked up as near to the caravan as we could. I should say here that someone had made the caravan and subsequently given it to Auntie Mill. It was made in a very amateurish way, the windows were made from twenty-five-millimetre soft wood with none of the necessary rebating, consequently when it rained the water ran down the windows and inside and on to the bedding, and that was what was happening now. However, we had no option, we all went in as quickly as we could, Mo laid Ruth on our bed while she got the three children ready for bed, whilst I got the cot which was also soaking wet, in from the car. I made it up, then got the mattress and the bedding in from the car. Finally, all three children were tucked up into the double bed and Ruth was in her cot. Because of the rain, the cot frame made Ruth's bedding wet and both double beds were also soaking. Mo and I were sitting on our bed. I just relaxed after the stress of driving in such horrible circumstances and getting ourselves settled in. Then I spoke out "It's good to be home." Did I just say that? Did I mean it? Yes, I did. And then another miracle was about to happen. During the day we would spend our time in the Manor House, Mo would be in the kitchen preparing vegetables and there would always be something that needed my attention. Ian Andrews, one of the fulltime evangelists, popped in. "I was hoping to see you" he said. He then explained that he and Rosemary, his wife, were shortly to embark on an extended ministry tour of the USA. 'Would we like to use their four-bedroomed house while they were away.' All he asked was 'would we make the mortgage payments whilst we were living there.' Of course, we jumped at the chance. *Miracle*

Looking back over that year, we realised how difficult it had been. Andrew Jordan even challenged me at one point, 'Are you sure it was right for you to come to South Chard.' 'Yes absolutely' I replied and he accepted my answer. Living at the Manor House was not easy, Aunty Mill ran a tight ship and for any of the many Christians who found themselves living in the Manor House at one time or another will be familiar with the expression of 'going through the mill.' She would spend her day in the kitchen, Mo would spend her days cleaning the house, changing the beds that weekend guests had used, washing and ironing and all the other tasks. Another couple, Vince and Pauline Matherick, were also permanent residents, at various times they lived in a house that belonged to Aunty Mill and then in one of the bungalows that the Purse's had inherited. Pauline was a tremendous support and I guess provided a shoulder for Mo to cry on many a time. During that year I made weekly visits to the job centre. At one time I went to one of the local supermarkets for a job offer. When they were aware of my experience in the food trade I was offered a job as Assistant Manager. It was explained that once I had learnt their procedures I could be offered a store of my own and was I prepared to move to a new location. We had moved to Chard specifically to join the church there and I was not prepared to move away.

Then I was told that the local bus company, Southern National had a vacancy for a driver. What did I have to lose. I went down to the local depot and spoke to the Mechanical Superintendent. He brought out a single decker bus and told me to get behind the wheel. He asked me if I knew the way to Crewkerne to which I replied 'Yes.' So, I drove to Crewkerne and back and his assessment was "You'll do, put in for your test, and by the way if you feel you want a bit more practice come and see me." Or course I wanted another practice run. Up until that time the largest vehicle I had driven was a ford Transit, a bit different to a forty-five-seater bus. I went back and he took me up to Coombe St. Nicholas and back. The day came when I was told to report to the Southern National garage in Taunton one hour before the test time. When I arrived, there was another person who had to retake his test. So, the time I had to drive, for the very first time, a double decker bus, was now only thirty minutes. Also, the other chap told me that the examiner would take me to a certain street in Taunton where the examiner would tell me to stop. Then when he had given me my instructions to proceed along the road I was expected to use the clutch to engage first gear, then move up through the gears, one after the other until I engaged fifth gear, without use of the clutch, and then repeat the exercise back down to first gear, again without using the clutch. What! I had never done that before, so he explained the principal of feeling the gear stick and judging the 'revs.' Sure enough the lamp post arrived and the examiner explained what I would behave to do. Then he said, 'carry on' and that was it. Amazingly I did it perfectly much to my utter amazement. [Miracle] Another Miracle! I drove back to the garage and the examiner invited me to join him in the lower saloon. Apparently, I had a few questions to be put to me. One was 'what shouldn't I do when driving a Public Service Vehicle (PSV).' I thought for a few moments and then replied, 'drive in a manor detrimental to my passengers,' "yes" he said "and what else." Again, I thought and gave an answer I thought would impress. Again, he made the same response, and then the next miracle occurred. Suddenly the word 'Smoke' popped into my brain and I blurted it out "Smoke." "That's what I wanted to hear, you've passed," he said. [Miracle] Nobody at Southern National explained that crew were not allowed by law to smoke on a PSV vehicle and now I didn't smoke anyway, it didn't even occur to me. It had to be another miracle! Then started a period of five days 'route learning' from Chard to Taunton, then back, on to Axminster and then to Bridport before returning to Chard. Also, to Crewkerne and on certain days of the week to Beaminster. Finally, to Taunton in a 'puddle jumper' the local term for a bus that only carried twenty-nine passengers. This route went via Coombe St. Nicolas, Buckland St. Mary and then Staple Fitzpaine and onto Taunton.

I found bus routes very strange, I knew I was heading for Taunton, which was the first route I took on my own. At that time, although I was heading for Taunton, we made several diverts to call at villages on the way. I was on a late shift and took over in Chard from the driver who had finished his shift. The bus was a single decker with fifty-three seats. By the time I got to Ilminster, I had just one passenger travelling all the way to Taunton. She was sat in the very rear row of the bus. Of course, I was nervous and getting behind schedule. I left Ilminster, got to Horton Cross where I diverted to Horton, then Broadway and onto Broadway Pound where I turned right. A lovely straight road as far as the eye could see. So, I increased speed in an attempt to make up some time. I went straight over a cross road, that I should have turned right at to go through Ashill. I glanced in the rear-view mirror and the look on the face of my female passenger was one of absolute horror. I could imagine what she was thinking, 'Where is he taking me, what's he going to do.' I immediately sopped the bus and explained I was a new driver and that I hadn't driven this route before and I reversed the bus and then drove to Taunton Bus Station without any further mishaps. On the route to Seaton we went through the village of Colaton which meant that drivers had to drive a fifty-three-seater bus that was eight feet two inches across a bridge which was just eight feet six inches wide. If you didn't line the bus accurately you would be in trouble; I managed to avoid it for a couple of weeks and by that time I was a bit more confident with driving the bus. Once, when driving to Burnham on Sea, we would drive along the sea front to the roundabout. Cars were parked where they shouldn't have been and made it impossible for me to turn around, so I had no option but to hit one, gently I might add as possible. The final episode worth telling, was when I was asked to work a Saturday rest day. After agreeing, I discovered I had to drive an old Royal Blue Coach down to Exeter bus station where I became a duplicate coach to London Victoria Coach station. I spoke to the leading driver and told him I had never driven a coach to London let alone Victoria Coach Station. I was told it would not be a problem, all I had to do was follow him. Which was fine for half an hour by which time he was far ahead of me. I do remember seeing a sign pointing to Earls Court and the Embankment which I took. I reached the north bank of the Thames and was just about to swallow my pride and ask if any one new the way to the Coach Station when I saw a sign pointing left to Victoria, and suddenly I was there. Good job the Lord knew where it was!

I had a new job as well. A firm from Croydon had set up a distribution centre in Chard. Situated in the old mill building in Bowden St, Woodpecker Pet Products supplied Pet shops in the west country. The manager lived opposite me in Ashcroft. He built up the first weekly round of shops and handed it over to me while he started a second round. Eventually there were three salesmen covering Somerset, Dorset, Devon, Cornwall, Gloucester and South Wales as far as Swansea and the Head of the Valleys Road. My lorry was loaded on a Saturday morning and I set out for South Wales on Monday mornings. My first stop would be Newport then I would make my way north through Cwmbran and then onto Abergavenny. Then I would make my way down one Valley and up the next valley spending the night in Barry. Then the following day I made drops in Port Talbot, Neath and Llanelli and Swansea. Eventually I was promoted to regional sales representative and spent a week concentrating on one round, each week working a couple or three days in front of the delivery day just getting orders from the shops and trying to push the special offers we were offering. But eventually the venture was shut down and the firm concentrated on its London area.

Our fifth child, Hannah, was born on the last day of July nineteen hundred and seventy-three, at Musgrove Park Hospital, Taunton. As usual, I had left on the Monday and was due back on the Tuesday blissfully ignorant of what was happening. Tuesday morning arrived and Mo and Teresa had had a falling out (again), by mid-morning Teresa had walked out. She was making her way to South Chard and hid behind a hedge whenever a car approached from the Chard direction. One car she recognised was being driven by Mike Ranstead, so Teresa jumped up and waved frantically. Mike stopped for her and bundled Teresa into the car and took her to the Manor House and duly handed her over to Auntie Mill. The help line was immediately activated, Kathleen Paine collected Teresa and kept her for the day. Another lady in the fellowship, who happened to be a midwife turned up and sat with Mo, assuring her that Teresa was safe and was spending the day with Kathleen. My boss was also advised and he decided to drive down to Barry in South Wales and took over the lorry from me and I drove his car back to Chard. The next day I drove Mo to the Maternity Ward at Musgrove Park Hospital and then it all became a bit of a rush. Mo was put on a trolley and wheeled into the unit, but labour was so advanced that there was no time to transfer her to a bed and Hannah was born on the trolley. As Mo was holding the baby she asked me 'shall we call her …..,' and here I have to be honest, I have now, after all these years, forgotten what we had decided. "No" I said, "How about Hannah," I quite expected Mo to say 'No!' It was so old fashioned at the time. But she agreed wholeheartedly. The girls were very excited, having another baby to play with. Ian was not so sure, he later confessed that growing up surrounded by four girls was too much and he hated them. When Hannah was three, we attended a wedding, at the site where the summer camps were held. It was a glorious day and tables were laid out on the lawn. Half full glasses of champagne were everywhere, and Hannah started a clean-up operation. She started to drink them and must have liked the taste. She quickly became quite drunk and was walking across the lawn staggering as she went with a wine glass in each hand and walked straight into a young fruit tree and promptly sat down with a leg each side of the trunk and the precious nectar clutched in her hands

The two girls were at Manor Court Junior School, but Ian was at Chard School. They were now old enough to walk themselves to School. One day I had left for work and Ian had been naughty, he had been punished with the cane. My mum was staying with us at the time and she gave Mo a right telling off, 'I never caned Phil.' Mo said to herself 'it might have done him good if you had.' Ian came home from school, he walked in the back door and apologised 'for being a bit late coming home but I heard you tell Granny that you broke the cane on my bottom this morning.' Apparently, the end of the cane had hit a dining chair and the end of the cane was split. Mo was explaining to my Mum that as the cane had slit at the end it would have to be replaced. The reason Ian was late was because he had knocked on the front door of the house opposite. When the owner came to the door, Ian asked him if he could have a new cane from the bush that was growing in his garden for his mum. My mum was dumb founded!

Soon after this incident we had been in the house for about a month when we were offered a three-bedroom council house. It was one of the houses that were being built on Holcombe and number 14 was ready to be handed over. We were faced with a dilemma, should we accept it and possibly put Ian and Rosemary in financial difficulties. In the end we realised that if we turned the council offer down it might be years before we were offered another one, so I had to contact Ian and tell him what we had decided. I was surprised that he just accepted it as if it was just something that happened. At that moment I learnt another truth of 'walking in the Spirit.' The realisation that God was in control of our lives. All we had to do was to believe and not to doubt when God worked the plans He had for our lives. So, we moved in and Ruth spent her first birthday in her seventh home. It was then I realised the significance of seven, God's perfect number.

We decided that in the summer holidays we would go camping at Praa Sands, which is in Cornwall. I made some boxes that fitted onto the roof rack which when we set up the tent would serve as tables and storage units. We arrived and found a pitch and set to erecting the tent and unpacking the car. It took us a good two hours or more. While we were in the middle of this a couple arrived with a caravan. They wound the jacks down, got the caravan level, erected the awning and were sat relaxing and drinking their tea. And we were still hard at it. I decided that camping was not for us, we needed a caravan. The only trouble was I couldn't afford one. It wasn't until the following spring that I had a dream that we were to buy a caravan and the word 'Panther' popped into my head. I got up and at breakfast looked in the local weekly newspaper and saw a whole page advertisement announcing a sale of brand new caravans that had been built to continental specifications but the order had subsequently been cancelled. The caravans were called 'Panthers.' Everyone I have asked who were or are caravaners have never heard of such a make. We drove to Warminster and looked at the range. We need one that would accommodate us and the four children. We found a caravan that was designed as a four berth, but each double bed included an 'L' layout which enabled a bunk bed to be fixed over the double bed. One was included as standard and we ordered an extra one for the other double. The cost was four hundred and forty pounds. They accepted our ten per cent deposit and was told we could have free storage until we required it. The forty pounds just about took our available cash, but we just had to trust the Lord. We went home and just expected the Lord to provide the balance, but the weeks went by and June arrived. Nothing! We naturally turned to the Lord 'Why Lord?' The reply was 'you haven't told the dealer when you want to collect the caravan.' So, I phoned the dealer and arranged to collect it on the Friday before the summer holidays began and could they fit a tow bar to my car on the day. It was all agreed, now all we had to do was just wait for the money to arrive. On the Thursday a cheque arrived from the liquidator. Finally, everything had been sorted. My life policy had been suspended and finally he was able to release the surplus funds to me - five hundred pounds. The Lord's timing is always perfect. *Miracle*

It was at this time that another member of the fellowship came to us. He was a school teacher and had just been appointed as a headmaster of a school in Bognor Regis. Would we like to buy his house in Chard? The price he was asking was very fair, there was no agents fees to pay and we bought his three bed, semidetached house in Ashcroft. The only problem was where to store the caravan. We were able to store it in the garden at Holcombe. I paid a visit to my farming friend at Green End and he was prepared to let me store the caravan free of charge.

Then a few days before Christmas, one year in the late nineteen seventies, we had an urgent phone call from Clive who was living in Montreal, Canada. His wife, Leslie was in hospital having just had a hysterectomy which had gone horridly wrong. Her mum lived on an island off the coast of Vancouver which made Mo the nearest and most accessible. I phoned a friendly Travel agent in London and explained the problem. He quickly phoned back with the question 'could we get up to Heathrow by nine am on Boxing Day.' We could, he had arranged a flight on United Airlines to New York. I asked about the Visa that would be needed. He said he was working on it. We arrived at the check in desk and her luggage was checked through, but she was not allowed to proceed as her visa was still being processed. Eventually it was approved by an official at the American Embassy. She was escorted by a stewardess to the gate and boarded the plane. Immediately the door was shut the plane started to move before Mo had reached her seat. When the plane landed she joined the queue for immigration when her name was called out. She was then escorted away. Mo told me later what happened. She was wearing her fur coat because of the North American winter and she could sense the crowd asking 'Who is this person who is getting preferential treatment' or perhaps being arrested and being catered away to Staten Island. Northing of the sort, her passport was stamped with a six-week emergency visa. Such was the speed her transfer made to LaGuardia airport she caught an earlier flight to Montreal landing an hour earlier than scheduled. She had to wait for Clive to pick her up and then walked into chaos and spent most of her time trying to clear the backlog of washing and ironing. When it was time to reconfirm her flight home, Clive insisted on paying for her flight. Mo refused saying it had all been taken care of. That was a bit of a leap of faith. At that time, I had not yet got the money for the fare. Clive took her out to a Chinese restaurant. As they entered all the clients were give a cloakroom ticket, and towards the end of the evening Mo's ticket number was called. She was given an envelope with $100(Canadian) written on the outside. Mo immediately said, "there's half of the ticket cost" and opened it up and to everyone's surprise not $100 but $200, in cash, was inside. Two miracles, flying with no visa and secondly the whole fare being supplied by The Lord. *Miracle*

Chapter 6

Summer Camps

Shortly after this I was invited by Uncle Sid to become a deacon. The fellowship was growing in numbers, and this was the first time the eldership felt the need for a diaconate. I realised that if I were to say 'Yes' I would need a job that could be worked around my commitment to the church. Then I saw an advertisement for a company based in Nailsea near Bristol. It was a franchise, selling greeting cards to newsagents, post office and general shops. I was allocated an exclusive territory which included the whole of Somerset and Bristol. It was suggested to me that I should plan to visit each outlet every three months. If there was a funeral or something else that needed me being at the church, if I was a week early or a week late it wouldn't make a lot of difference. Cards were sold in boxes containing a gross of cards and the suggested mark-up by the retailers was one hundred percent. More importantly, when I needed more cards I would drive up to Nailsea and pay what I had picked up on the previous visit. So, a box of cards that I sold for ten pounds would be sold for twenty pounds and I paid the distributor five pounds.

One of the Sunday school teachers took about forty children away for a week-long bible camp in Sussex. Two Christian ladies who both worked in London, had a cottage in Sussex where they spent most weekends. They were also visitors to the fellowship in South Chard. They had a large paddock and a copse with a stream running through it. The appeal went out for tents we could borrow and apparently the Sunday school children had a fabulous time.

I was not involved in the outreach the first year, but I was invited to get involved in the administration and setting up the following year. All the applications for places came to me and I soon realised that we would need tents for fifty children. Many of the frame tents we had used the first year were no longer serviceable, so out of the fees we charged I bought five ex-army ridge tents. These were large enough to sleep ten children and two tent officers, who, in the main, were Christian university students who were able to offer their services free of charge in return for three good meals a day and lots of hard work.

At this time, meals were prepared in the tiny, tiny kitchen of the cottage and meals and the meetings took place in the garden room. It was a tight squeeze sitting forty children around the tables for meals, in fact if it was nice and dry the staff eat out on the patio. Over the years we eventually had a total of nine ridge tents and a thirty by twenty foot marquee, which when it was not being used were stored in one of the garages at South Chard fellowship. We levelled the area where the marquee would be sited, laid out some four by two timbers and screwed sheets of chipboard to make a level floor, where we could put the tables and benches out for meals. Then in the evening the tables were folded up and stacked away for the meetings.

We were allowed to bring the piano over from the house. I remember one week in particular when young Gill Greenwood was playing the piano and leading the worship, there were so many youngsters dancing that the floor was bouncing up and down that I and another staff member had to hold the piano to stop it falling over.

We had our difficult times as well. In particular the owner of the field next door was very opposed to us being there. On the first night we would stress this to everyone that his field was definitely out of bounds. Of course, it had to happen. One of my tent officers noticed a couple of lads missing. They reported this to me and I organised a search of the camp site, but we found no trace. We eventually found them in the field next door, so not wanting to disturb the meeting I took them into the lounge of the cottage where I gave them a severe talking too and gave them an option, either they could take my punishment, (This would be three of the best with my cane) or I could take them straight home, right now. They both opted for the first option, which I knew they would. I also knew that one of the lads was prone to easily cry, so I decided to wait until the meeting finished, it also allowed them time to reflect on the seriousness of their actions and to prepare themselves. As soon as the meeting finished I said to the other boy 'let's pray, you have to ask the Lord to forgive you, and then when you are ready just let me know. Then as he did so a tent officer walked in and observed what happened next. I did what I did at home with my own children. I administered three stipes with the cane, and before he could cry the cane was thrown to the floor and I had gathered the lad into my arms and was loving him and both of us were crying. I had purposely left the more emotional boy until last. I was hoping he would learn something from the actions of the first boy, which I am glad he did. He did and took his punishment like a man. My friend, Ron, was amazed, he confessed to me he had never witness punishment so sensitively administered. I replied, 'it wasn't punishment, it was correction.' The end of the story followed when I got back to South Chard and told the father what I had had to do. He quite understood and said if ever the lad wouldn't do as he was told, I would be called for. I never had any trouble with him. In fact, he grew up to be part of the music group in the church.

On another occasion, another lad went missing, we eventually found him fast asleep draped over a bough of a tree. Another time, one of the helpers walked over the manhole covering the cesspit, which broke in two and he landed in about four feet of you know what. We promptly got him out and hosed him down none the worse for his experience. There were plenty of stories like this.

I would have to arrange a weekend working party and hire a lorry to take the tents, marquee and all the trestles tables and benches that were borrowed from the fellowship. Also, the number of camps increased eventually to four weeks for the children and one final week for all the helpers and university students. The kitchen facilities were still a problem. With the permission of the owners of the cottage we applied to the local planning authority for a timber frame building to be granted for ten years, which could be renewed. I immediately wrote to the parents asking for two things, would they ask their fellowship for donations to be sent to the fellowship at South Chard and secondly to ask for volunteers to help build. We immediately arranged a working party to prepare the site and lay sewer pipes and installed a plastic sewer tank. Next, we put the shuttering in for the concrete base which was to be fifty feet by twenty-five feet wide, which required about fifteen cubic yards of pre-mixed concrete. This would be delivered in three lorry loads on a Saturday morning. We travelled on the Friday evening and erected a tent and we were up first thing to receive the first lorry load and the other two loads came in two-hour intervals. Then a few weeks later the timber frame building arrived and was erected by the company. One of the features was the huge support pillars that were made out of four by two timbers that were assembled, glued and pressed by a specialist company in Sweden. The actual building was forty-five feet long by twenty feet wide, with a veranda. It was quickly erected but we still had loads to do and kitchen area had to be fitted out. On one of our journeys up to Sussex we stopped at a Little Chef for coffee. Around the back was a stainless-steel commercial grade double sink unit. I enquired about it and was told that we could take it away for nothing. And so, a monthly programme of work parties commenced. The kitchen needed fitting out with work spaces and a store room created. At the other end of the building the toilet block was built and an office for me and a store room. Then there were the electrics to be sorted out. Fellowships sent volunteers with just the right skills. All I had to do was to make sure the materials were delivered to site. Each month I gave the invoices to the treasurer of South Chard Church, Mr Ben Smalldon. It became obvious I was following in Sid Purses footsteps. Never had a budget, nor how much money was available just trust in the Lord.

Eventually it was finished. Mo who was now back teaching at the local comprehensive school would come in the front door of the house at the end of term, we kissed on the door mat and I would be up in Sussex for the next six weeks. One of the weeks Mo would come up and head up one of the catering teams. What had started out as a holiday for our own young people grew into a country wide series of camps in July and August. Nancy Roberts led the ministry team, there were Bible studies every morning. After lunch there were various games or a trip to Hazelmere or Petworth. If the weather was kind we would organise a picnic by the river at Midhurst. A lot of the children wanted to be baptised in the river. One of my friends from South Chard performed the baptising one week and he shared that standing in the river for nearly an hour nearly froze his feet off. As I would be the one standing in the river the next week I made sure I asked the

Lord for his protection. Before we baptised any child, we would always seek parental consent. On one occasion that involved me phoning the father of a child, who was a missionary in India. He was only too pleased to give me his permission. Many years later I met the lad, now a full-time evangelist with the Don Double organisation.

Eventually the Lord showed us it was time to transfer the management of the outreach to the local Christian Fellowship based in Petworth. I left my caravan on site, it was still used for ministry there. I had given of my time for the six weeks of the summer holidays, together with the time taken in administering the booking procedure and of course spending working weekends the project involved. Not once did I seek payment because I was 'doing it unto the Lord.' However, the fellowship took up an offering for me afterwards and I can honestly say that the Lord knew my needs.

Chapter 7

South Chard

South Chard Fellowship was always reaching out and a couple, Derrick and Thelma Reeks suggested that we should hire a holiday camp for a week. As a fellowship, we had a ready supply of speakers and we had a wide number of fellowships who made a point of visiting us at various times of the year. The Leadership agreed and Derrick approached Butlins. We held one at Clacton and then moved the venue to Bognor Regis. I was asked to head up the stewarding and I got a team of about twenty to monitor the various venues. The evenings were the high light of the day with Ian Andrews or Harry Greenwood being the main speakers. There was always an alter call for salvation and physical healing and many people were saved and indeed healed of various ailments. Then on the final evening a collection was taken for the ministry. On one occasion Harry led the prayer for the offering. When he finished he followed it up by saying "If you don't know what to give, just sign a cheque and we will fill it in." I said to myself, 'No Harry, you can't say that' but it was too late. The buckets were sent around and then collected and were taken to a room where we stewards started to count what had been collected. Then someone held up a cheque saying, 'I've got it.' I took the cheque and told everyone to stop what they were doing and asked them all to reach out for a figure for the amount to enter on the cheque, then I asked everyone to reach out as I prayed for the unity of the spirit and a unity of amount. Eighteen of the twenty wrote twenty pounds on the piece of paper in front of them, which I then collected. I realised that this could be an excessive amount for some or an insulting small amount to another. I went to the Butlin administration office and found the cabin number of the person and I spoke to the lady. She was quite happy with the figure the Lord had shown us. *Miracle*

Vince Matherick then approached me. His tour business was expanding and his wife Pauline was struggling with all the paper work spread out on their dining room table. There was a small cottage attached to the Manor House and I presumed Auntie Mill had agreed to let Vince have it to use as an office. Would I like to join the company? We agreed a salary and we put two desks in the office and a filing cabinet. My first job was to introduce office procedures and tour costing guide lines and put the business on a firm footing. This always was difficult. Vince had a heart of gold and sometimes his generosity ran away with him.

I worked with him for a number of years. However, when Israel and her neighbours were fighting, the bookings just dried up. I realised Vince couldn't afford to pay me, so I went back to driving buses. As soon as the tours picked up, I stopped driving the buses and picked up where I had left off. Eventually Fellowship Tours had grown and we were able to take on a school leaver, Hayley, a member of the fellowship. I was to spend a time in Israel, making as many as six trips a year. Some were purely business, inspecting hotels and arranging prices for the following years. The thing I enjoyed the most were leading the tours. One of the earliest ones was a school party from Manchester. I had gone up to the school, which was a girl's catholic school, and talked to the girls and their parents about the benefits of a visit which led to a group of forty girls and teachers signing up for the tour. I thought my work was done but the head teacher insisted that I accompanied them. On the way home, I thought about this and decided that I would be like Ali baba with his forty girls and I needed a chaperone. When I got home I spoke to Mo about joining me on the tour. She wasn't a bit keen, in her eyes all we would be doing would be visiting a lot of churches and ruins. What could I say to persuade her. I came up with Abraham's journey from Haran to the Promised Land. Every time the Lord blessed Abraham, he raised a pillar of stones as a memorial and that as we visited various churches, that was would we would be doing – remembering the words or actions of Jesus. So, she came. On the second day we stopped at a small church known as Dominus Flevit situated on the Mount of Olives overlooking the Temple Mount. The Latin translation means Jesus Wept over the city (Luke 19:41-42). The school had arranged to celebrate Mass there so Mo and I waited outside. A Priest came up to us and asked why we were standing outside, so I explained that we were not Catholics, he responded 'We all worship the same Lord, do come in and join us.' It became a very moving experience for both of us. Later on in the tour we visited the Mount of Beatitudes, and before we went into the church I was asked to explain why we were there. The story is told in the Gospel of Matthew chapter 5 and listed nine different type of people who Jesus called blessed if they did certain things, like Blessed are the poor, who mourn, are meek. I have not a clue what I said but just read the account and tried to explain it as simply as I could to the girls. Afterwards Mo said I spoke for about half an hour, that many of the girls had been weeping and quite a crowd had gathered to listen to what I was saying. Many years later we had a big party there which filled two coaches, we left and were making our way back to the hotel in Tiberius when we realised we were missing one gentleman. We enquired of the other coach, and no, he wasn't on that coach either, so we turned around and went back and found him watching a convoy of tanks being transported to the Golan Heights. He was lost in prayer, praying for the Peacemakers, who shall be called 'sons of God.'

Many are the stories I could tell of Israel. I remember taking a mixed group who had responded to press advertising. Two, who joined were Catholic priests, and after supper on the first evening I took them and a few others for a short walk around the neighbourhood and at one point I stopped and explained that on the other side of the wall was the site known as the Garden Tomb. "What is that" one of them asked. I realised I had made a mistake because for Catholics the tomb is situated in the Church of the Holy Sepulchre, so this couldn't be the tomb. From there on everything I said was treated with suspicion – my theology was at fault. When we got to Tiberius I asked the guide if we could stop at the beach belonging to the Church of Scotland. There is nothing there to link it to a religious site, but just a nice quite place to pray. We all got off the bus and did just that, we had a time of prayer. The priest who had questioned my theology walked away from the group and later on in the bus he sat by me and apologised for walking away. Then he told me that he had been in the ministry for some thirty years and while he was walking along the sea shore had met the Lord for the very first time in his life.[Miracle] Can you imagine my excitement? I immediately spoke to the guide and arranged that the next stop on the programme would be St Peter

Primacy on the shore of the lake. This site commemorates the disciples, having fished all night and caught nothing, being invited to partake of the fish that Jesus had caught. After the meal Jesus invited Peter 'to feed my sheep.' I invited this new Christian to share his testimony, meeting Jesus just half an hour ago. On another occasion we drove into the Golan Heights to Caesarea Philippi – one of the sources of the Jordan River. It is a very peaceful place set in a National Park. We had been there about thirty minutes when an Israeli army officer approached our guide, who then came to me and said it was time to get on the coach, which we did except one elderly lady who was engrossed in picking a posy of flowers. I went to her and stressed it was time for us to be on our way. Only the guide and I knew that the army were about to start shelling the Syrians, and within five minutes there would be incoming fire.

Although Israel was our main destination I went on a fact-finding trip to Egypt to find out if eight-day tours there would be viable. I flew in to Cairo and immediately caught the connecting flight to Luxor. I visited the temple of Karnak and the Valley of the Kings and visited several hotels. I then returned back to Cairo travelling on the overnight sleeper train. I stayed in a hotel very near to the Pyramids, which I rode around on horseback with a guide. The next day I was taken to the Cairo Museum and a coach tour around the main sights of the city. The following day I caught a coach transfer to Port Said where I was due to take a cruise liner to Ashkelon in Israel. Although this had been agreed with the tour operator in London the instructions hadn't filtered down to the ship. It fact there were four tour ships in port but by the time the Egyptians officials were prepared to stamp my passport the last ship was sailing north towards the Mediterranean Sea. My guide and I jumped into a launch. We caught up with the ship and I had to stand on the gunwale of the launch with a briefcase under my arm and a suitcase in my hand and jump onto the accommodation ladder on the ship. *Miracle* I landed in Ashkelon the next morning and made my way into Tel Aviv. The next exercise was to get back to Egypt by coach via the Gaza Strip. My luggage was examined by the Egyptian customs officers and immediately all of the promotional material I had picked up in Egypt was confiscated. I immediately complained to an officer looking on and it was restored to me. When I was in the army we had a phrase for the type of bloke 'clifty walla' at least that is what the Arabic sounded like. It meant someone who would steal anything.

Mo and I went on a trip to Greece to research the footsteps of the Apostle Paul. We landed in Athens and hired a car and spent a day looking around the capital - the Acropolis, built on the top of Mars Hill with the Parthenon, the Agora and the Temple of Zeus and the changing of the guard at the Presidential Palace. We stayed in a hotel in the Port of Piraeus, which as a place to stay was much nicer that Athens itself. Next day we headed north for Thessaloniki and the port of Kavala, the place where Paul first landed in main land Europe. We then drove to Philippi where he delivered his first sermon. His first 'convert' was a 'seller of purple,' a lady called Lydia. Next on our itinerary was Berea, which is about forty-five miles west of Thessalonica. Paul preached 'with much success' (Acts 17:10), in the local synagogue. Tradition tells us that in order to protect the ancient synagogue it was surrounded by a tall wall which hid it from view and we were led through big wooded doors to have the history explained to us. We then started to make our way South West towards Meteora. A formation of rock pillars in central Greece which became the site of six monasteries precipitously built at the top of the immense natural pillars in the local area. It was the location of the James Bond film 'For your eyes only.' We stayed a night at the small town of Kalabaka, before making our way through the tobacco growing area of Greece to Delphi, considered by the Greeks as the navel, or centre, of the world. The most important site here is the site of the ancient Oracle, and the Sanctuary of Apollo. It was here that every four years, athletes from all over the Greek world competed in the 'Game' starting in 586 BC.

Our next stop was Corinth, which meant we had to drive over the bridge spanning the Corinth Canal. Initially proposed in classical times, a failed effort was made to build it in the 1st century BC. Construction was started in eighteen eighty one and was finished in eighteen ninety three. The ancient city of Corinth was where Paul spent eighteen months with Aquila and his wife Priscilla who, like Paul, were tent makers. Both Mo and I came to the conclusion that this journey of Paul's had entailed constantly being chased out of every town that he had visited, and probably needed a good rest.

Chapter 8

Mum and Dad

Mum and Dad.

The partnership Mum and Dad went into when they bought a camp site in Berrow didn't work out. My parents bought a two-bedroomed bungalow in Stratton, near to where they started their married life. However, they were getting on in years and decided to move nearer to us. They bought an 'upside down' bungalow in South Chard. By that, I mean the lounge were upstairs, because it offered the best views, and went down to the bedrooms. Soon after this move, Mum's health began to deteriorate, and one day she decided to go for a walk. Dad was down in the garden, and after a couple of hours went to check on Mum. Imagine his horror, when he found her missing. We immediately phoned the police because she was wearing a short-sleeved dress and the evenings were getting chilly. Eventually the police found her with a posy of flowers she had been picking not far from Forde Abbey, about three miles away. She was taken into Tone Vale hospital at Cotford St. Luke for a check-up and to give Dad some respite time. However, whilst she was there, she had a fall and broke her ankle, and had to remain in hospital until it mended. Apparently, she couldn't be discharge until her health was as good as when she went in, and of course her memory was deteriorating all the time. Dad was worrying as to how he would be able to look after Mum when she was discharged. Mo and I were more worried over Dad's health, so we suggested that if he were to sell his bungalow and we sold our house we could buy a bigger house where we would be able to help him look after Mum. He was relieved and agreed immediately. We bought a three-story semi-detached house with five bedrooms and an attic room, in Crimchard. We immediately started working on the property. The first job was to convert the single bedroom on the first floor in to a kitchen/diner, and as soon as that was finished Dad was able to move in. The front double bedroom became his lounge because the views were stunning, all across to Glastonbury Tor. The rear bedroom would be for Dad and eventually Mum, when she was discharged. But she wouldn't be, she died in the hospital in September nineteen seventy-seven. Meanwhile I continued working on the second floor. When we bought the house, there were two double bedrooms and a large 'L' shaped room, which I made into two single rooms and a second bathroom.

Dad continued to live with us. He spoilt the grandchildren no end. The favourite treat was at bedtime, after the kids had cleaned their teeth, they would go down stairs to say goodnight to granddad who would give them sweets.

Dad would drive his Renault R8 down to the town once a week to get his shopping. On one occasion he came home and threw his car keys on our kitchen counter, saying "That's it, I'm not driving anymore." Apparently, he had scraped one of the wings getting the car out of the garage, and then had a minor scratch with another car in the town carpark and then misjudged getting the car back into the garage.

Having ridiculed me for most of the time over my Christian faith, imagine my surprise, when one day he asked us if he could see uncle Sid, the Pastor of our church. A few days later the two of them were in dad's kitchen chatting over a cup of tea, when Dad suddenly asked Sid 'What do I have to do to be saved, should I take communion.' Uncle Sid came down and asked if we could get the necessary bread and wine which I took up. Uncle Sid got dad to say the sinners' prayer and they shared communion together.

About a month later Dad was admitted to East Reach Hospital in Taunton to have his cancerous prostate removed. However, the pre-op assessment showed that Dad also had lung cancer and advanced brain cancer and it was decided he was too ill to undergo surgery and was transferred to the Palliative Care ward at Cheddon Road Hospital. We went to see him every day and, on the Friday, we noticed that Dad was rubbing his arm and grimacing. Mo asked what the matter was and Dad said 'my head hurts.' I went and asked a nurse about Dad's condition. She told me that the brain cancer had advanced and was now causing confusion and Dad didn't know where he was hurting. Mo and I discussed this, and we came to the conclusion that as Dad had acknowledged Jesus as His Saviour, there was no reason for him to continue with ever increasing pain and discomfort. I prayed that the Lord would take Dad into Heaven. The next day we had a phone call from the hospital. Dad had died on the twentieth of December nineteen hundred and eighty, peacefully in his sleep during the night. *Miracle* At church on the following day, I related what had happened and testified that the Lord had answered my prayer. A few moments later a chorus started and a lot of folks were dancing and I joined in, much to Teresa's disgust. "How could I possibly dance when Grandad had just died." He was buried three days later on Christmas Eve.

Chapter 9

Julia

Julia.

Julia had moved into the flat on the first floor, where Dad had lived. She met a fellow, John Glass, who had just completed a degree in environmental science at Plymouth Polytechnic and was now working on a farm on the outskirts of Chard. He started attending the fellowship and before you knew it the two were going out together. They were married on the seventh of May nineteen eighty-three and set up home in Honiton, Devon. In time she became pregnant, but unfortunately, she miscarried. It was an ectopic pregnancy which also meant that one of her ovaries had to be removed. Despite this they went on to have two sons, Adam and Stuart. Stuart was born in Taunton hospital. It was nearly Christmas when Julia went into labour and then the snow fell and completely threw the whole country into chaos. Eventually the roads here in Somerset cleared, but as we got to Kent the area was still in the grip of snow drifts everywhere.

John was teaching in the local secondary modern school and Julia had enrolled at the University of Greenwich studying Business Studies with German. She started her dissertation with the sentence. 'My father always said 'Je suis Anglais, je ne parle pas Francois.' In nineteen ninety-eight John applied and got a teaching post at a school in Somerset, which was the Lord's timing, because we should shortly be needing their help. (See chapter on Ukraine) By 2010 his mother's health was deteriorating and they decided to live with her, so he could take care of her. John was not fit to work at this time, and Julia managed to get a part time position as the administrator of a community centre in North Bristol. John's mother eventually died and her house was sold so John and Julia moved into an apartment. With his share of the estate he formed his own transport training company. He would give employment to young men who were 'on the dole,' teach them to drive a lorry and thus get them into permanent employment. It was about this time that Julia was diagnosed with breast cancer. Following surgery, she had to have a course of chemo therapy. Her local Primary Care Trust (PCT) was one of the few that did this in the patient's home. Mo suggested that Julia come and live with us for the week of the treatment, which meant that Julia would get the support she needed at that time.

John's business was not as successful as it should have been, and financially they were struggling. It was becoming ever harder to pay the rent. Eventually they had no option but to move, so I suggested to them that they should come home and live with me. I knew John didn't like the idea of it, but I suggested they put their names down on the housing list with the local council. Julia's health was fine, she was in remission, and was busy trying to find employment, without any success. They were with me for thirteen months before they were offered a council property in Winsham which they accepted, and then the following week Julia secured employment at a firm of Accountants in nearby Chard.

Chapter 10

Teresa

Teresa.

In nineteen seventy-nine, Teresa was living in Swindon and training to be a nurse. She was very fond of a boy who attended the fellowship we had attended there. However, I heard through the 'grape vine' that he had moved into Teresa's flat. I drove up to Swindon and confronted the pair. If they loved each other, they should get married, but apparently, they didn't, so he moved out and went home. Meanwhile, Teresa's health was suffering and she had to give up nursing. She got a job as a nanny to three young children of a divorced Greek Cypriot. He relocated to North London and eventually to Cyprus and settled in Nicosia. Teresa went with him. They planned to get married; Mo and I, together with Mo's sister, Meg, flew out for the wedding, which took place in July nineteen eighty-one. Whilst we were there I took the opportunity of teaching Mo to swim and more importantly, Mo led Meg to the Lord.

Teresa's marriage lasted for ten years, during which they had relocated back to London. After the marriage ended she lived with a chap in Kent for two years, during which he turned violent towards her. To quote her words. "I can tell you a miracle that happened. George had a knife at my throat and was going to kill me, and in my head, I cried out, 'Please God help me' and George flew across the room and hit the wall and turned to me and said, 'it's not worth it' and went and locked himself in the bathroom, which is where he still was when Julia arrived." *Miracle* Quickly the girls packed Teresa's clothes and then left. Julia phoned Mum and she phoned the bus company. They sent an inspector out to Winsham and he explained the situation. He took over my shift, and I drove the bus back to Chard, picked up my car and with Graham, my son-in-law, drove to a pre-arranged stop at a Little Chef on the A303, while Mo stayed at home continuing to pray over the situation. It took quite a while for Teresa to get over the episode. She took her PSV test and got a job with Southern National and met another driver, Colin. They married in nineteen ninety sixty and have been very happy ever since.

Chapter 11

Ian

Ian.

Ian won a scholarship to Wellington School when he was eleven and completed his education there. He was seventeen and went to camp for the last time. He took a fancy to one of the girls who came from London, so he decided to move to Brixton, and he got a job at a petrol filling station. He found a bedsit but eventually he realised that the girl was not interested in him. Also, he wanted to see more of the world and loved Israel. He decided to up sticks and moved to Israel. He was fortunate to get a placement on a Moshav. This is similar to a Kibbutz where everyone works according to ability and is paid according to his need. So, a young man might be expected to work a seventy-hour week and be given his accommodation, food and laundry taken care of and be paid pocket money only. A Moshav is a collective of small holders who each have their own plot of land and are free to grow what crops they like. Then the farmers come together to market their produce collectively. One of the bungalows were made available for the volunteers and in the main they catered for themselves, mainly from what was being grown around them.

Eventually mail was being forwarded from London addressed to Ian. One of them was from a Bank who was seeking reimbursement of an overdraft that Ian had run up before he left. Unfortunately, at the time he flew out to Israel he didn't realise he owed any money to the bank. I took advice and wrote to the manager of the bank explaining I was the father of Ian and that I would make period payments into the account as I could afford it, without accepting liability. Then after Ian had been in Israel for about seven months I felt that I should visit him. I talked it over with Mo and we both felt that Ian was worried about the debt and how he would face coming home with a cloud hanging over his head. I didn't want to spend a whole week visiting him, but I also knew that the minimum stay in Israel was six nights. I approached one of my contacts in London and explained that I wanted to fly out for half a week. He struggled to find me a flight but came up with a flight out of Gatwick going to Eilat on the Wednesday and back from Tel Aviv to Gatwick on the Sunday. Perfect.

I arrived in Eilat in the early evening but had to find my way to the Moshav which was about ten miles north of Jericho. The only option that was available was to catch a bus to Tel Aviv. Then catch a bus from there to Jerusalem, and finally catch the first bus in the morning going to Tiberius, via Jericho. Eventually I arrived at my destination, and walked up the road to the Moshav entrance, where I explained to the guard at the gate that I was visiting my son. He let me pass and as I approached the administrative part of the Moshav, a lady approached me and stopped to ask if she could help me. "Yes" I said, "I'm here to visit my son, Ian Nowell-Smith." She nearly collapsed with shock. She had told Ian over breakfast that during the night she dreamt that I would arrive at the Moshav in the morning. *Miracle* They both laughed at the possibility and Ian went off to the fields. She explained that Ian would be back at her bungalow at about three, he was pruning the grape vines and would be bringing the cuttings in with him. I explained my long journey, so she showed me where Ian slept – in an air raid shelter and I thankfully fell into it and slept until Ian woke me.

I explained that there were no ill feelings between Mo and I, and that he would be welcomed whenever he decided to return. We then walked up to the farmers bungalow where we spent the next few hours carefully slitting the vine buds down the middle of each bud and repeating it on every bud on the stem. Then she would examine each one under a microscope and count the numbers of grapes in the cluster. By doing this to every bud on the stem and repeating the procedure on all of the other stems she would arrive at the best level of pruning for the whole field to give the optimal crop next year. We continued this on the Friday morning and finished work at midday, it was the 'eve of Shabbat.' I phone a Christian Arab who managed a hotel in Bethlehem and asked if he could accommodate Ian and I for two nights. "Of course, my friend, you are always welcome here."

We got there and we were taken up to the roof where a BBQ was being prepared for us. The next day, we caught a bus into East Jerusalem and we did some sightseeing, wandering into the old walled part of Jerusalem at the Damascus Gate and into the Muslim quarter. Eventually it was time to catch the bus back to Bethlehem, for the evening meal. Next day after breakfast it was time for both of us to head back to Jerusalem, I to catch the bus to the airport, and Ian, the bus back to the Moshav. Sunday was a normal working day for him. We gathered our luggage and I asked my Arab friend how much I owed for the stay. Nothing, my friend, you are always welcome here. Then I realised, the staff had been brought in specifically to care for us. I was to realise in later years, this is typical Arab hospitality. *Miracle*

He had had his work visa extended once and now it meant he would have to leave the county. He bought a return ferry ticket from Haifa to Cyprus and stayed with Andrew and Teresa for one month. He went back to Israel, and the Moshav for another six months, to help with the harvest. During his time in Israel he saved sufficient money from his earnings to pay the air fare and he flew home. He had been home about two weeks, when Val Winyard knocked on our door. She and her husband were members of the Fellowship and offered Ian a job as manager of the recording business they owned distributing cassette tapes for the blind. This led to him getting a diploma in business studies. He met and married Cindy, who lived in Ilminster. Later he joined the Police force and after his training was stationed in Farnham, Surrey. They had two boys, Alex and Chris. Cindy wanted to get back to Somerset and eventually Ian transferred to the Avon and Somerset force and moved into a police house at Almondsbury. Later on he was posted to Taunton, during the time we were in the Ukraine. John and Julia had moved into our bungalow, but eventually bought their own house, just in time for Ian and Cindy to move in.

They joined the local Baptist church and then disaster struck. I think that both Ian and Cindy realised their marriage was on the rocks. They were eventually divorced. Ian had bought a house in Creech St Michael and part of his job with the police was training new police volunteers and he was eventually promoted to sergeant. He met, Gemma, who was serving in the Dorset Police and he applied to join Dorset police and was accepted. They bought a house in Dorchester and Gemma was accepted into the Dorset police as a beat officer in Dorchester. Meanwhile Ian did a spell working out of Weymouth in the custody suite and also as a patrol officer, then a spell in the force headquarters at Poole. He then joined Firearms and as a sergeant headed up one of the armed response units. He then moved back to Weymouth as a custody sergeant there. Ian is now retired and working in a comprehensive school as a stand in teacher.

He and Gemma have one daughter, Taya who is now twelve years of age. Alex is engaged to Harriet and are planning to get married soon. Chris is now living in Plymouth and studying to be a marine engineer project manager and working his placements working on Royal Navy ships.

Chapter 12

Ruth and Hannah

Ruth.

In the Spring of nineteen eighty-one when Ruth was ten, (which would made Hannah nearly eight years old), the two of them decided they would cook Mum and I a birthday meal. They prepared a menu and had placed it on the table, along with napkins and place settings. Then when it was ready they called us into the dining room. None of us can remember what we ate, however it was a 'proper meal,' not baked beans on toast. For dessert there was Baked Alaska. This puzzled Hannah, she couldn't understand that ice-cream could be baked in the oven and remain as ice cream, but when it was served, she certainly tucked in to it. I should add that Mo and I were not allowed in the kitchen and looking back I am amazed that not only did Mo trust our ten-year-old, but together with her younger sister to cook in the kitchen unsupervised. They did very well and as a reward I presented them with a plane ticket each to Israel. Ruth's immediate response was 'Dad always gives us his old plane tickets.' Hannah exclaimed that it 'has OUR names on them, they're real.' Ian, who was fourteen at the time, was also included in the trip.

Eventually the summer holidays arrived and the children had the time of their lives, although Hannah was a bit young to take it all in especially why Jesus had to die. I tried to explain it while we were on the Temple Mount. I explained that God had ask Abraham to kill his son as a sacrifice to God. I explained it in this manner. 'One day, in Heaven, God and Jesus were having a conservation about how wicked people had become.' God proposed the thought 'If I were to send you, Jesus, to die for all of mankind's sin could I bear the grief.' Jesus replied, 'I don't know if I could bear the pain and sin.' Then God said, 'Let us watch Abraham and his son Isaac.' And so, God spoke to his friend Abraham and told him to take his son, his beloved son to a mountain and sacrifice Isaac. They set off on the three-day journey and as they got near to the mountain Isaac asked his father 'Where is the lamb?' Abraham replied, 'God will provide.' God watched as Abraham laid Isaac on the alter and took hold of the knife when God caused a lamb to be caught in a hedge – God had provided the Lamb and he knew that Abraham trusted God. Also, Jesus knew that Isaac trusted his father, Abraham. Thus, Jesus knew he could trust his Father. They had to wait about two thousand years until the time was right.

We took a day to visit Bethlehem and visited the Shepherds Fields with its distant views of Jerusalem. Then we returned to Manger Square and the Church of the Nativity. We ended up visiting my friend Abu and his sons who are Christian Arabs and owned a gift shop in the town. Immediately Abu saw Ruth, he offered me six camels to purchase Ruth because of her blond hair, highly prized by Arab men. He also wanted to adopt Hannah and she was quite taken by the idea at the time. We made sure we brought them both home.

When Hannah was twelve, Mo was a supply teacher at her school teaching Home Economics. At the end of the lesson, Mo set the class some homework. All of Hannah's friends turned to her and said, 'she's your mum, tell her we don't get homework in this lesson.' Hannah did and Mo's response was totally without emotion said "Well now you will have something to remember me by."

When they both got home, Hannah got properly told off and was instructed to <u>never</u> do anything like that again! And she didn't.

Hannah worked in the Chard branch of the Nat. West bank from nineteen eighty-nine until she relocated to the Crewkerne branch in nineteen ninety-one and she moved in with a girlfriend at the same branch. Then in nineteen ninety-four she was moved to the Taunton branch and moved back home, soon afterwards she met Neil. They were married in the august of nineteen ninety-seven and had two sons.

Tony was born in July two thousand and one, on Neil's birthday. Nat was born three years later.

One morning Tony woke up and complained of chest pains. Hannah took him to the doctors and was immediately sent to Musgrove Hospital in Taunton for a precautionary x-ray. He fainted at the end of the procedure and was admitted to the paediatric ward. He was discharged at around midnight with strict instructions to return for more tests in the morning.

By eight p.m. he was admitted to the Cardiac care ward at Bristol Children's Hospital. He had excess fluid in the sac that holds the heart and about a pint was drained off. However, the sac filled with fluid again and as the fluid was again drained it was noticed that there were bits floating in the fluid. So, Tony had to have open heart surgery to correct the problem. He was now diagnosed with viral pericarditis

Neil and Hannah started a book keeping company, and, although the company had grown, both of them were offered better positions with two companies. Neil became the accounts manager of a kitchen manufacturing company, and Hannah with a media research company where she is now the finance director. Unfortunately, their marriage didn't last. Hannah and the two boys moved out into a rented property, and Neil and Hannah eventually divorced. Hannah eventually met Ian and they were married in Banff National Park, Canada in Two thousand and seventeen.

Hannah.

Chapter 13

The Ukraine

Mo and I had travelled to Ontario, Canada for the first time in nineteen ninety-five. At the time there was a big church, Airport Vineyard, near to Toronto Airport, which we wanted to visit, purely out of curiosity. I asked Clive it he would like to take us at some point. "No, but you can take my car." This was my first visit to North America and the journey would entail driving along route 401.

When we got to Toronto the motor way was eleven lanes each way, with vehicles over, and under taking us at what seemed like breakneck speeds. I don't know how, but we reached the church safely. I don't remember much about the service, but afterwards we strolled into the bookshop. My attention was drawn to a cardboard carton with a sign saying 'free, help yourself.' Naturally, I did. I picked up an out of date copy of the Jewish Chronicle, a newspaper published in England. I don't know how it got to be in this particular church in Canada, but the lead article leapt out of the page at me. It told the story of an Englishman living in Hull, Yorkshire, who was helping Jews who were living in the Ukraine to make 'Aaliyah.' This is the Hebrew word which describes the process of Jewish people returning to the country of Israel. I knew the man! He was a church leader in Hull and had approached Fellowship Tours to organise a pilgrimage to the Holy Land for his church members. As I read the article I discovered that the charity known as Project Exobus (a play on words with Exodus, a book in the Old Testament, and the coaches that were sent out to the Ukraine to drive the Jewish people to the airports in the Ukraine) needed coach drivers, and I was a coach driver. I was struck by all that the Lord had to do to get my attention.

We had to make a visit to Canada at the right time; the Jewish Chronicle was on the shelf, free. If it hadn't been free I probably would have passed it by. We had travelled three thousand miles west to find out about something that was happening in Kiev, the capital of the Ukraine, three thousand kilometres to the east of where we lived. Finally, I knew Phil Hunter, who headed up the project. I knew, without a doubt, the Lord was speaking to me and Mo was supporting me all the way.

When we got home I looked at the finance that I would have to raise; our house still had a mortgage to be paid and together with other expenses I calculated we would need to raise ten thousand pounds. Next, we met with the Pastors of the church and explained what we felt the Lord was asking of us and how much money we would have to raise. I don't know if this amount of money was too daunting for them, but their advice to us was to 'wait and test the word of the Lord for twelve months.' We agreed but continued to move forward. First, we arranged an interview with Phil Hunter in Hull where we learnt a lot more about the project. I had to take a driving assessment which was satisfactory. Mo would be able to accompany me. We would be based in the far eastern region of the Ukraine in the city of Kharkov, where they had a team house which Mo would run.

We came home and shared it with the children. At that time Ruth and her husband, Graham, were living in Colchester. Graham was a corporal in the Royal Army Ordinance Corps (RAOC). Ruth spoke to her Pastor and we received an invitation to share our vision. As a result, we came away with a cheque for six hundred pounds and a pledge for two more instalments of the same amount. I contacted a Messianic Jewish friend who I first met at the house fellowship we both belonged to in Swindon. He was now married and living in Kingston, Surrey. He wrote back explaining his father had just died and he had just received an inheritance from the father's estate and included a cheque for one thousand pounds. In two weeks, we had raised a quarter of the amount, such an encouragement!

Then Julia and John came to talk with us. John would be starting at his new school in the August and could they live in our house while we were away. With a few more gifts from friends the whole amount had been given or pledged inside six weeks. [Miracle] We met with the Pastors and told them the good news, I don't think they expected the

Lord to act so quickly, but we did assure them that we would honour the promise we had given them regarding waiting the year.

In the spring of nineteen hundred and ninety-six we moved up to Hull. We were accommodated in the team house there and I spent the next six weeks learning the basics of coach maintenance, and as the need arose, driving a coach for the private hire arm of the parent body, Good News Travels. I particularly remember two episodes. The first was we took two double decker coaches across the Pennines to Manchester with Bon Jovi fans going to a concert at the Manchester City football ground. My fellow driver and I walked around the neighbourhood where we had parked the coaches. I was amazed at the derogation and the amount of barbed wire running along the top of the rear fences of so many houses; prostitutes hanging around on street corners and drug dealings being conducted so openly. The second trip was so much better. I took a group of school children to a training establishment for agricultural students. I tagged along with the party and I was particularly interested on the pig rearing unit. They had a large heard of sows and thus lots of piglets. These were kept in pens of similar ages; each animal had their ears tagged and they would go to one of several feed dispensers. The ear tag would be read and if the animal was due a feed, the appropriate amount would be dropped into the feeding tray. In this way the growth of each piglet was monitored with the correct feed according to the age of the pig. The aim of the game was to rear a pig that had a minimum about of fat and would grow and progress on to the next pen where the food had been changed to meet the next stage of growth. This would produce the best pig in the shortest time possible and sell for the best price at market.

The time arrived for us to leave. The coach was loaded with aid, food and clothing that would be donated to Ukrainians in both Kiev, the capitol, and also in Kharkov. Some of the food would also be used by the teams in both cities. With me was a Dutch volunteer, who was a fully trained vehicle mechanic, and Phil Hunter. We drove down to London and onto the Embankment where about twenty people were joining the coach. They were going on a factfinding mission and they came from various support groups from across the county. Then we made our way to the M25 motorway with a brief stop at a service area where we loaded more supplies of aid to be distributed in the Ukraine. Then it was a mad dash to Folkstone to catch the ferry to France. Phil phoned the ferry company and they held the ship just long enough for us to board the ship, which was already heading out to sea before we even disembarked the coach. Our destination: Oostende.

We spent the first night at the home of a Belgian supporter before heading for Berlin, where the local Christians had gathered to hear Phil talk about the project. I was fascinated by the translator. He kept his eyes on Phil and not only translated Phil's message into German, but he also mimicked Phil's gestures and mannerisms. He was brilliant. The next day we continued our journey through the former state of East Germany and onto the Polish border. We stayed on the outskirts of Warsaw, in a farm house. The couple, very sincere Christians, had heard a message that there would be days coming when Christians would have to flee for their lives. As a result, they built a dormitory with accommodation for about thirty people. We three chaps stayed there for the next two nights, while our fellow travellers stayed at a nearby hotel. The next day we toured Warsaw, visiting the area of the former Ghetto, and the headquarters of the Jewish uprising against the Nazi's in nineteen forty-four.

After this brief interlude, we drove on to Lublin, a Polish city very near to the Ukrainian border. We stayed there for the night and the next day we visited Majdanek, one of the smaller Nazi death camps, where an estimated seventy-eight thousand Jews died. We were taken into a barrack room that had metal cages all around the outside walls and a double bank down the centre of the room. These were a metre high and filled with shoes, according to size and colour. I immediately realised that one pair of shoes probably meant a life. We also went through a pair of big doors into the gas chamber, with the nozzles still in situ under the roof. I was so relieved to walk out of the door into fresh air. We were then shown the remains of the cremation ovens and finally a memorial that had been set up on a pile of ashes, which was about five or six feet high, where we had a time of contemplation and prayer. Mo was a bit susceptible to all of the ash, so she walked around the circular memorial and was surprised to see a lower jaw on a child partially covered by the ash. She believed!

We approached the border and the queue to cross stretched for what appeared to be for ever. A man approached us and asked if we needed assistance to get across the border. We had met our first gangster who apparently could achieve almost anything for a price. We turned his offer down and as a consequence it took us about five hours to reach the border point where our passports and visas were examined. We were through and we had one more stop to make. We deposited our passengers at a local hotel and then drove to a 'styanker,' Ukraine for secure compound. We paid the nightly charge parked up and went to the cafe for a meal knowing the coach and its contents were safe with armed guards constantly patrolling the park. The next day we arrived in Kiev. We unloaded some of our cargo and the following day I travelled on to Kharkov on another coach, driven by a Belgian volunteer driver, and a Dutch girl, Fenny. They had just delivered a group of Ukrainian Jews to the airport, who would be flying out to Israel to start a new life in the Promised Land. Fenny and others like her were Ukrainian speakers, and their role came to be known as 'fishers,' (In Matthew chapter 4 verse eighteen Jesus said Peter and his brother Andrew 'Follow me and I will make you fishers of Men') who would visit synagogues and clubs and talk to them about relocating to Israel. They would escort them to Kiev to get their exit visas which they would need to leave the Ukraine. The law was that permission to leave the country had to have the written consent of the parents of both sides of the families.

We got to our destination after an eight-hour drive. Some volunteers from England had put some extra bedrooms in the roof space, so we now had three single rooms which were occupied by Fenny and two girls who came from east Germany. Mo and I were shown a self-contained flat with a double bed and a small kitchenet and a shower room. So, this would be our home for the next twelve months. On the ground floor there was also another single room for the driver, a kitchen diner, and a huge living room, which was mainly used as a store room. Our larder was situated in the kitchen and was accessed by lifting the trap door and climbing down into the cellar, which was about six feet square.

Two doors down the dirt road live a family who were a huge support for us. We needed a telephone which was apparently virtually impossible to get. The answer was our neighbour placed a cable through the trees. He would answer all phone calls and if it was for us he would press a button which rang a bell in our kitchen. Then one the girls, all of whom spoke Ukrainian, would answer the phone. This was to be one of my major tasks, to get our own telephone line installed. It took me about six months when one day I was summoned to the telephone office and I took Fenny as my interpreter. We were told that the installation would cost one thousand US dollars. I relayed this information back to Hull and was told to go ahead. Next time we went to Kiev we came back with the money. I arranged to visit the boss at the telephone headquarters and I was told to come to his office at nine the next day. We were kept waiting for half an hour and were finally shown into the boss's office where we handed over the money. We were then told that all the engineers had left for the day, and we would have to come back the following day. It suddenly dawned on us, a further payment was needed, a bribe, to get the job completed. The next day I went back, but this time I went with my neighbour. Once again, we were kept waiting and then were told that all the engineers had left. I said it would be no problem; my friend would bring the wire into the house for me. He went outside and lifted the manhole cover outside and we threaded the wire through and coupled it to the phone. Suddenly it rang, and we realised the phone engineers in the local exchange had connected us, which saved us a trip to the exchange to do the job ourselves.

The whole economy was in tatters; inflation was so rampant that a new currency, that had been printed in Canada, couldn't be put into use, so a temporary set of notes were used, which were called coupons. When we filled the coach with diesel we would first have to pay for the fuel and then the pump would be switched on and off when we had the correct amount of fuel. It is the only time I have felt like a millionaire, because it took that many coupons to fill the fuel tank. I don't know if it was true, but we were told the reason for this mess was that employers were supposed to pay Central Government the same amount in taxes as they paid their employees in wages. The way around this was not to pay their staff and so Central Government didn't get their due. The staff were paid in kind, so as you entered a city you were made aware of what that city manufactured. Women lined the roads, trying to sell bath towels, zinc buckets and cooking pots. I felt very sorry for those who were trying to sell pencils! Our other neighbour's son fell and cracked his head open and needed to have the wound stitched. His mother ran around to us, could we drive them to the local hospital. She explained that if she called the ambulance service it would attend but the crew would demand five US dollars, and if it wasn't forth coming they would drive away again. She didn't have any dollars but her son needed to get to the hospital. Of course we took them, waited for them and brought them home. The next day she came around to the house again, but this time she had a big enamel bowl full of sugar. We didn't need it, but she insisted and we had to accept the gift graciously. We bagged it up and distributed to those who needed it in a different neighbourhood. It was unwise to advertise our presence more than necessary.

We had also brought about a thousand Christmas shoe boxes, so we arranged to visit three different orphanages over the Christmas period. The first one was for children who had been abandoned, their parents just couldn't afford to keep them. The second was for crippled children and the third was full of children with mental health issues. It was heart breaking. I gave one of the crippled boys a box which he opened and inside was a pair of slippers. It was a joy to see his face light up. However, they were quickly taken away, the pair was far too big for him, but another child had been given a pair that was far too small. Both boys were now happy again.

The incident that upset me the most involved an elderly couple who were house bound. A Polish charity had arrived in Kharkov and were giving out twenty-five kilo sacks of potatoes and some dried food meals to Jewish people. We agreed to take the identity cards of the couple and we joined the queue. Many of the Jewish folk who were queuing gave us some funny looks, but Fenny explained why we were there, so everything was ok. At the time, if you were Jewish your identity card was stamped with a large 'J' in the top right-hand corner. My thoughts went straight to the Holocaust when six million Jews were killed in death camps. I had just made myself a target. In fact, in nineteen ninety-six, Boris Yeltsin was seeking a second term as president. One of the other candidates was reported to have said 'Vote for me, and I will solve all of Russia's problems, I will open up the gas chambers again.' I don't know if that was true, but Yeltsin won his second term.

Shopping in the main, was conducted at an open space near the main cross roads about half a mile from the house. Mo would walk down and quickly learnt enough Ukrainian to buy bread. French sticks were very popular, and Mo would ask for six, pronounced as 'shist batona.' Fish arrived in a lorry, with a water tank, and live fish would be fished out with a net. Chicken portions arrived in the morning deep frozen in twenty kilo boxes. In winter individual portions were hacked off with a hammer and chisel. We were very selective in summer, with temperatures in the high thirties, the chicken quickly thawed out, and any left over at the close of business would be put back into the deep freeze and brought out again the following day. Not good!

The Chernobyl disaster occurred on the twenty fifth of April nineteen hundred and eighty-six. The river Dnieper flows through Kiev, but starts in Smolensk, Russia, and flows past Chernobyl. So, to ensure the team had good water to drink I would drive to a nearby forest where there was a spring. I would collect between one hundred and one hundred and fifty litres in Coke bottles and take the bottles to Kiev each time we went.

Driving in the Ukraine was challenging to say the least. We moan about our pot holes. We had to contend with some up to a foot deep. We would drive on both sides of the road to miss the worst, only returning to 'our side' of the road when we met another vehicle coming the other way. Another problem were the Police. Because our vehicles came from a variety of European countries, they carried German, Dutch and UK number plates. The police would assume we were rich, and so we were frequently stopped. The favourite offence was to have tyres of a different manufacture. I was shown to have one Dunlop tyre while the rest were Michelin. Or course if I paid the 'fine' or offered a carton of cigarettes, I would immediately be on my way. The problem was that the police would contact the next station where

I would have to pay the fine again. So, we just played it out. I would tell the police to speak in English, I had 'nyet Ruski,' the girls would keep quiet, and when possible give me an update. Most times it meant a delay of about half an hour without succumbing to a bribe. Only once the police won. We were stopped at an important cross road and my Belgian colleague was driving. He went into the office and was told that we were guilty of damaging state property. A police car had reversed into an opening and the officer was leaning on the bonnet, the coach drove through a puddle and the officer's uniform was soaked. It was my time to go into the office. I took my interpreter in but told him to keep quiet. We were quickly outside where I was told that the rule book I had been shown to emphasize our crime was indeed a Russian book of growing vegetables. If we wanted to get home that day we had to pay the fine, we had a whip round and just managed to raise the fifty US dollars requested and then we were on our way.

Whist we were there, Teresa and her husband, Colin flew into Kiev and spent a week with us. They came with us on one of the trips taking those Jews who were starting their journey to begin a new life in Israel. Afterwards Teresa told me she felt so privileged to have witnessed the work we were doing. She spoke to one old gentleman and how he had served with the Russian army during the Great Patriotic War (world war 2), he was proudly wearing his medals. He was overcome by the kindness shown to him on our journey to the airport. We gave him a cup of tea. He confessed that this was the second time in his life that anyone had done him such a kindness. The first time was when one of the girls had taken him to the Israeli Embassy to get his papers in order that he would be able to leave. An Embassy official had also offered him a cup of tea. He became so emotional, he started to weep just because the tea was free. We are so fortunate to live in such a country as Great Britain.

Our friend Sereosha had erected a metal fence around the property. There were hundreds of metal panels two metres high and fifteen centimetres wide. I had asked him if we could use them to make a perimeter fence. Yes, he would get straight on with it, but did we have a ladder. I was puzzled, why did he need a ladder? He had an electric welder but needed the ladder to be able to reach the power cables, in order to clip the welding apparatus onto the overhead power cable before it reached our electricity meter. Typical of the way the Ukrainians approached things. It was finished before Teresa and Colin arrived, and Colin spent a lot of time painting it. Teresa especially was shocked by the fear she could see in the people around her. Mo sent her to the market to buy the daily six French sticks. Teresa approached the little hut with just a small opening where you would speak to the lady inside, money would be passed through and the goods passed out. Very few people made eye contact and those who did, their eyes were 'dead.'

We also took them to church on the Sunday morning. Church officially started at ten thirty, but a lot of us realised that the musicians practised for an hour before, so we started getting there at that time as well. Why miss an hour's worship! We had joined this particular fellowship because the pastor was an American evangelist, and so he preached in English. This meant we got the sermon first hand while the locals had to wait for the translation. On one occasion, he was sat in the congregation whilst the musicians led the worship. When he felt it was right he would make his way to the side of the stage area, but then the musicians started up another chorus and Bill, (the Pastor) turned around and walked off. A little later he walked on to the stage again and took one of the mics from a singer, when once again another chorus began. Bill gave the mic back and continued to walk across the stage and off the other side. On the third attempt he was successful and was able to give his message. This was followed by a time of ministry to those who needed prayer, and 'church' finished when the last person had been prayed for. The time had gone by so quickly we didn't realise it was four thirty in the afternoon. The service had lasted for seven hours.

One Sunday a lady came and sat next to me and all the way through the service she played Tetris on her mobile phone. On that particular Sunday we celebrated Holy Communion, and Bill explained that we should take a piece of bread and hold it until everyone had been served. This lady took a huge piece and started to eat it straight away. I mentioned this to Bill at the end of the service, and he explained that she probably had heard the music and had come in out of the cold. In a few weeks after she had been discipled, everything would be different. Bill and Igor, who was the lead musician, had a discipleship class going on every week, training new comers to the Christian faith. After six months training, many of these new Christians would be sent out to local villages to spread the gospel. Bill, his wife and four children first set up an outreach programme in Moscow, before moving to Kharkov. He approached the city officials requesting a venue to open a Christian church in the city. Repeatedly he was turned down. The local Russian orthodox church was very much against the idea. In one of Bill's meetings he mentioned he liked the 'blues music.' 'Why didn't you say so before, of course you can have a venue,' and so the church was born. Igor was also a lover of 'blues music' and became the first convert. Bill's only son married a local girl and their eldest daughter married a local lad, and today they still lead the church there. Bill sent his wife and two youngest girls back to America, while Bill followed the Lord's leading and relocated his missionary outreach to Kabul in Afghanistan. By all accounts he was so successful in converting Muslims to Christianity that the Taliban placed a Fatwa on Bill's life. He therefore started a discipleship school in Northern India and took his Muslims converts with him. Once they were trained up, they were sent back to Kabul to recruit the next class of disciples of the Lord Jesus.

I had plenty of projects that Phil Hunter had lined up for me. We needed a garden shed and the ground was 'prepared'; a shallow trench was dug and soft sand tipped into it and levelled, and then thoroughly wetted and trampled on. That was the foundation! Next came the brick work. Sand and cement were mixed, and that was it. I rushed into the house and brought out the washing up liquid which turned the sand and cement into mortar.

Phil decided a workshop was needed at Kharkov and there was room to build it in the garden. The first job was to create a driveway from the road into the garden, and down the side of the house. Obviously, it was standard practice to dig out the top soil and then fill the excavation with soft sand which was then thoroughly wetted and trampled down. Next a heavy mobile crane arrived, quickly followed by lorries loaded with pre-cast reinforced concrete slabs each six metres by three metres wide. In total six slabs were laid and the drive was completed in one day. This allowed the workshop to be brought in. It was semi-circular in shape, wide enough to get two coaches in, with an inspection pit to the left-hand side. The shape of the roof left plenty of space down the sides for work benches.

Our year long stint was coming to an end. We drove our last party of Jews to the airport and then the following day started on the long trip across the Ukraine, Poland, Germany and Belgium. Our first hiccup encountered was at the Ukraine Polish border. The Ukrainian custom officer, realising this was his last chance to get a bribe insisted that the driver's sleeping quarter be emptied, which I duly did, and then we waited for the officer to come back. But we waited and waited, when about four hours later I saw that he was preparing to go off duty. I approached him and he said 'oh, you can go.' All of Good News coaches had been fitted with long range fuel tanks and when we got to the German border, at Frankfurt an der Oder, the German customs officer insisted in dipping all three fuel tanks and insisted we paid the import fuel tax. It had started to rain as we left Kharkov and it continued to rain for the whole trip. The River Oder was about to burst its banks and we were one of the last vehicles to cross into Germany before the road was closed because of flooding. The rest of the journey passed without incident, and when we docked at Folkstone, there was our son-in-law, John waiting to drive Mo and I back to Taunton.

Chapter 14

Mo's Illness

We arrive back home from the Ukraine in November nineteen ninety-seven and had Fenny stay with us over the Christmas period. Our grandson, Samuel, was born on Christmas day. Mo became unwell after the new year. She was constantly throwing up, and was not able to keep anything down, not even sips of water. Because of the time of year, we had a series of home visits from three locum doctors who all gave anti sickness tablets. I took Fenny up to Luton airport on the Saturday, the fourth of January for her flight back to Holland. Ruth, who lived opposite us at the time, was going to keep an eye on Mo.

After I left, Ruth spoke to Mo, she was very concerned about Mo's health and the lack of action on the doctors' part. Ruth wanted to call the NHS Health Line. Mo made her promise not to ask for an ambulance. On calling the health line, Ruth was put through to an Emergency doctor at the hospital. She explained Mo's symptoms and asked at what point do the medical staff consider her condition serious. The doctor responded and said he was sending an ambulance straight away. Ruth had not asked! When I got home Mo was just being loaded into the ambulance. Teresa went with her and I followed in my car. Mo was quickly diagnosed with Salmonella food poisoning and admitted. After seeing mum settled, Teresa and I drove home. On the Sunday I went to church in the morning, then after lunch went into the hospital to visit Mo for a couple of hours. Then at about ten in the evening I had a phone call from the Hospital, Mo had had a major stroke and I was advised to come into the hospital as soon as possible. I made a quick phone call to Teresa and also to my Pastor, the Reverend David Goodyear, who also came into the hospital. The doctor explained that Mo was also complaining of a head ache and it was feared that Mo had contracted Meningitis and was taken straight to an operating theatre. It was there, whilst on the operating table the stroke happened. If you are going to have a stroke, that was the best place to pick. Help was immediately on hand. By the time we got there Mo was back in bed in a side ward, so we had privacy while we prayed for a positive outcome for Mo. I and the rest of the family continued to visit Mo every day and on the Thursday Jennie Metcalfe and I visited Mo in the morning and went to the restaurant for lunch. We got back and the door to the ward was locked. It was the quiet time, and we had to wait for about fifteen minutes. We had been sitting by the bed just a short time when Mo had another stroke. We were asked to leave while the staff looked after Mo. Eventually we were allowed back in and we sat with Mo for quite a long time. Mo was paralysed on one side of her body and she was very weak. The nurses had to move her every few hours to avoid getting bed sores. To slate her thirst, we dipped a cotton bud into water and let Mo sip the water. Eventually Jennie went home but I stayed until nine o'clock in the evening. The nurses had settled her down for the night and sleep was a good healer.

The next day, Mo had three visitors. First was our daughter who sat by the bed side and prayed that angels would come and minister to her Mum. The next visitor was a member of the fellowship and was also a specialist cardiac nurse who popped in to see Mo during her lunch break, she also prayed that angels would minister to Mo. The last visitor was Doctor Andy Adams who was a pathologist at the hospital and had also visited during his lunch hour. Both staff were wearing their white coats so Mo immediately said to Andy "I'm not ready to see you yet" and he laughed and then also prayed that angels would minister to Mo.

When I went in in the evening Mo related all that had happened during the day. Again, I stayed until nine o'clock until after the nurses had settled her down for the night. The lights in the room were turned off, the curtains were closed, but some light came in from the corridor outside. Gradually Mo started to drop off to sleep, and immediately Mo saw six men standing around the bed with a seventh man standing by Mo's shoulder. He was point to each man in turn and then to parts of Mo's body and he was mouthing words, but Mo could not hear what he was saying. She opened her eyes but the room was empty. Once she closed her eyes, there they were again, so she just laid there with her eyes closed, fascinated. Eventually she dropped off to sleep. The next morning, three nurses came into the room to help Mo sit up, give her a wash and to help her with her breakfast. Can you image their surprise, Mo was sat up in bed! "Who has been in and helped you to sit up." "Nobody, but during the night, the angels came in and ministered to me." *Miracle* The three nurses spun around and bolted out of the room. Mo described the scene, visually it reminded her of a children's comic book. The ward doctor, a Spaniard, came in, sat on the bed and said, "I hear you saw angels during the night, tell me everything about them." Not a word about her recovery. Eventually he left and apparently phoned his family in Spain to relate the experience. He also showed Mo the text book on strokes. It was about three inches thick, but Mo's stroke, that had been caused by dehydration, was so rare there was only two paragraphs on the condition. As a result, Mo was visit by medical students from hospitals all over the west country.

From that day her recovery was quite spectacular. I was allowed to take her out to the hospital chapel in her wheelchair and she was amazed to see a small bronze statue of a baby nestling in the palm of a hand. It was there to be something tangible for parents who had experienced an infant death. To Mo, it was exactly what the Lord had shown her in a vision she had had during the night. Isaiah chapter forty-nine and verse sixteen says, "See, I have engraved you on the palms of my hands." (New International Version). Although she had difficulty walking, still need help dressing and having her meat cut up, she had made sufficient progress to be discharged home rather than spending time in the stroke rehab unit.

Ruth and her Husband had relocated to Creech St Michael and lived in a small two bedroomed cottage less than one hundred yards from our front door. Their second child, Jessee was about two years old and whenever she had a strop with Ruth, Jessee would announce "I'm going to Nanny's" and Ruth would have to make a quick phone call to Mo and warn her of the arrival of Jessee.

Mo and I had discussed what was best for the future. We were very grateful of all the help and support the nurses had given to both of us while Mo was in hospital, but there is a limit to the number of boxes of chocolates we could give them. We decided that I would approach the Ambulance Service, and so I became a voluntary car driver. This paved the way for me to give up my carer's allowance, and Ruth became Mum's carer instead. As I explained earlier, Ruth's cottage had two bedrooms, so Graham and I converted one of the two bedrooms into 2 bedrooms, one for Jessee and the other had a bunk bed for the eldest boy, Tim and the youngest, Sam.

A year after the stroke, Mo and her friend Jennie went to a Christian Prayer training event in the Brecon Beacons. During the Saturday evening, Mo was prayed for, for complete healing. In Charismatic fellowship churches it is not unusual for someone who has had 'hands laid on them' and prayed for, for that person to fall to the ground. This is what happened to Mo. Her legs gave way under her and she started to sink to the floor, but someone behind her gently lowered her to the ground. As far as Mo was concerned, she 'came around' and started to get up. Imagine her surprise, she thought she was on the ground for about fifteen minutes but was told it was forty-five minutes. The next morning, she was preparing to go down to breakfast and reached for her walking stick but decided to leave it in the bedroom. She sat down at the breakfast table when Jennie joined her. Jennie leant over to cut Mo's bacon and then explained "What are you doing?" Mo was already cutting her bacon. During those forty-five minutes Jesus had worked a miracle, she had been completely healed. The mobility scooter I had bought for her was sold off.

Over the next two decades Mo spent much of her time in prayer ministry, while I continued working as a volunteer ambulance car driver. We were both very much involved in helping Marilyn Baker, a blind, Christian, singer song writer and her companion Tracy Williamson. Initially, I took over the administration of her holiday retreats at Christian run hotels in Devon, Kent, Dorset, and in South Wales. One particular event took place at Green Pastures in Poole. I had worked out the bed allocation but didn't realise one couple really did need a ground floor room. The wife had suffered a stroke but hadn't made a note on the booking form. By the time I realised the problem the hotel was completely full. The couple were very gracious, and the lady would go up and down the stairs on her bottom. Marilyn had persuaded Mo to share how the Lord had completely healed her of the effects of her stroke. Afterwards Mo talked to the lady privately and asked her if she would like a time of prayer. Yes, she would so they went upstairs to the couples' bedroom. Mo prayed with her and then suggested that she should walk the length of the bedroom unaided several times, and each time she did Mo could see the improvement in her stature and ability in walking. So, Mo suggested that they go down stairs. The lady said she wanted to get her walking stick, but Mo said that she didn't need it in the bedroom so leave it on the bed. They went down and into the garden, and can you believe it, she started to run around the garden. The Lord had completely healed her. [Miracle] What was Mo's reaction? She just wanted to fade into the back ground, not to take any credit for what had happened, just to give all the glory to her Lord, Jesus.

One of my all-time best photos of Mo.

Chapter 15

Surprises

Over the years I had planned various surprise trips for Mo. One of the first was back in the nineteen eighty-five, we packed the children off to school and then drove down to Exeter to look for a new car. We spent most of the day going from dealer to dealer and it was about two thirty and time to head home to pick up the children from school. I headed for the Motorway but took the wrong exit and we were heading for Cornwall. "Where are we going. You are going the wrong way. We'll be late picking up the girls." Then I had to explain that I had arranged for Ruth to stay with her friend Jane Carter. She lived just three doors away. Hannah was staying with her friend Jackie Dunning who also lived very near to us in Crimchard. Also, we were driving down to Cornwall for the weekend. Mo remonstrated "I haven't packed any clothes." 'I have packed some clothes; the suitcase is in the boot.' We were on our way to St. Ives for the weekend. We came home having had a lovely time, except for one thing – mum was very unhappy, and Hannah explained it thus, "mum made us girls promise not to allow dad to pack for her, if ever he did this again. It turned out that dad had packed all mum's pants that had no elastic."

We would have great times at Christmas. After we got home from church the children were sent off to find presents that had been hidden all over the house. The only exception was the kitchen, which was out of bounds, so I could get on with cooking the lunch in safety. Then we sat down to dinner and when it was time to serve the Christmas pudding I asked Mo if she could bring it in. "Where is it?" she asked. "It is on the kitchen table," I replied. "What, under the Towel?" came next. "Yes!" Mo lifted the towel and the pudding was in the microwave, which we didn't have the day before, which was what she had be longing for. It was a complete surprise to her. As was the automatic washing machine that replaced the twin tub and the tumble dryer that replaced the Flatley drier on another occasion.

In nineteen ninety-two we decided to take a long weekend trip to Holland and visit a flower festival that is held every ten years in Zoetermeer. I said to Mo that it would be nice if she and I, together with Ruth and Tim, drove up to Chatham in Kent and spent the weekend with John and Julia. Somehow, Tim must have heard about a boat ride and kept on 'when are we going to get to the boat.' I decided to go around the M25 'clockwise.' Just north of the tunnel under the River Thames, a new service area was being built, but in the meantime, there were a couple of portacabins that were pressed into use as a temporary service area. The outside of which had been painted as an image of a cross channel ferry ship. Tim was satisfied and nothing else mattered. He had seen his ship. But now it was time to explain where we were really going. Not to Chatham, not to John and Julia's for the weekend, but to Holland for the weekend and our destination was Sheerness. John and Julia were waiting for us and then Mo started to say, 'what a pity Hannah couldn't come with us.' I had to explain that Hannah couldn't get the day off, which was true. She was, however able to get the afternoon off. Hannah takes the story. "I left at lunch time and bombed up the Motorway and just made it in time to board the ferry. Mum had already been surprised by firstly, a different destination and secondly John and Julia turning up to join the party. Mum was already crying with emotion before I got there and when I arrived, mum's reaction just hit me! I think her exact words were 'you said you couldn't come. Please tell me there are no more surprises, I can't take any more.'"

We were married on the Saturday August the sixth. In two thousand and five we celebrated our forty fifth wedding anniversary, which also fell on the Saturday. I arranged with our pastor to hold a special celebratory service in which I rephrased the vow I made to Mo all those years ago: ......from this day, for better, for worse, *and we have had wonderful times and disastrous periods,* for richer and poorer, *and we have certainly come though those periods,* in sickness and health. *And I had faced being scarred by fire and Mo had had her stroke,* and we promised still to love and cherish our love until death.

After the service Mo and I drove off. What Mo didn't realise was that there was a reception planned at Ruishton village hall, to which I had invited as many friends who were able to come. We hurried over there where the family had laid out tables and chairs and a cold buffet meal. As each guest arrived we had a photo taken of us greeting them.

Mo's final surprise came in the December of 2012. Every year, for several years now, we have a family Christmas meal at a pub or restaurant, where all of us try to get together prior to Christmas day, as we are not usually together on the day. This particular day it was being held in the pub in Norton Fitzwarren, not far from where we lived. Nearly everybody was there. It had been a hard few months for Mo, as she was trying to be supportive of both Julia and Meg, her sister, who both had cancer. There had been set an extra meal setting at the table, but we didn't think too much of it. Then a bouquet of flowers were brought in by one of the staff who gave it to Julia. The card read something like 'just to let you know I am thinking of you, but I really would like to give you a hug, so stand up and give me one.' Julia stood up and told John to stand up and give her a hug, thinking the flowers were from him. They weren't. At that point Ruth walked in and surprised us all. Mum was very surprised and over the moon. Ruth wanted to come and show her support not only for Julia, but for Mo especially as she was supporting Julia and Meg. Ruth was just in the UK for a long weekend, as she had to return as Hannah was visiting them for Christmas.

Chapter 16

Decision Time

Not exactly a surprise, but Ruth came for a chat with Mo, which she related to me. Basically, Ruth suggested we should sell our bungalow and they would sell their cottage and buy a house between us. I could understand why she suggested it, their children were growing kids and where they lived they had no garden what so ever. I didn't want to move, after all things consider, the bungalow was supposed to be our retirement home. I had designed it for the two of us, and I did a huge amount of the internal work myself. I said, 'No way!' However, I slept on it and by morning time, I realised that they needed the extra space, and in years to come, they would be on hand to look after us. So, my 'No' became a 'Yes.'

Eventually we found a suitable house a mile up the road in Creech Heathfield. It had four double bedrooms, two bathrooms, two reception rooms and a large kitchen/diner with a walk-in utility room. Outside were garaging for four cars. These would become our Granny annexe. We constructed a large bedroom with an ensuite shower room and a walk-in wardrobe. We also created a small lounge with our own front door, a guest bedroom with an ensuite toilet with an additional access to the garden. Just as we were finishing it we had a visit from the council. 'Were we going to have our own kitchen?' 'No' we replied, 'we we'll be eating with the family.' So, we didn't have to pay any additional council tax.

Can you imagine our surprise, when Ruth once again came to talk to us with news that once again would affect our lives? They were planning on emigrating to Canada. My immediate reaction was 'what was I to do with six bedrooms, three reception rooms, three and a half bathrooms and nearly half an acre of gardens. Ruth immediately said, 'Come with us.' Mo said, 'That would mean having immediate access to one daughter and three grandchildren and leaving behind four children and seven grandchildren behind.' She considered that too big a price to pay.

Ruth and Graham went over to Ontario, in two thousand and five for a week to get their plan firmed up and to be sure that was what they wanted. In two thousand and seven they went again for a 2-week holiday with the children, but this time to Calgary, Alberta, where they would live. Mo and I also went with them. Graham spent a couple of days with the Calgary police department and we also went house exploring. They eventually settled in an area of Calgary called Somerset. We extended our stay by another two weeks. When they flew back, Mo and I joined the tourist train from Calgary to Vancouver which took us over the Rockies which included an overnight stop at Kamloops. We had one night in Vancouver before we boarded a cruise ship on an eight-day cruise to Alaska. In those two weeks we enjoyed enough vistas and animals to last us a life time.

We got back to Vancouver our eldest daughter, Julia, had arranged to meet us at the hotel. The next day we hired a rental car and drove across the Rockies taking three days on that part of the journey. We showed Julia were Ruth and Graham planned to live before heading south to Medicine Hat in Southern Alberta to pick up the Highway 1, as it is known in the 4 western provinces of Canada, or the Trans-Canada Highway across the rest of Canada, which would take us right across Canada to Kitchener Waterloo for a short visit with Mo's brother, Clive and his wife Leslie. Again, more life long memories of places visited as we drove through Saskatchewan to Regina. Then into Manitoba and Winnipeg before turning south at Kenora and to cross into the United States at International Falls in the State of Minnesota. Here we turned East again because we all wanted to visit Mackinac Island in Lake Huron. It was the setting for the film 'Somewhere in Time' which starred Christopher Plummer and Jane Seymour. The island is less than four square miles with less than five hundred residents but hosting as many as fifteen thousand visitors a day during the peak season. There is an almost total ban on motor vehicles, except a police car and a fire engine. The acceptable way of getting around is bicycles or horse carriage.

We carried on to Sault Saint Marie where we entered Ontario, Canada. Just a day's drive to our destination of the twin cities of Kitchener Waterloo. It was a long day's drive and we drove through a terrific thunder storm with blinding rain and really strong winds. We were driving though a small village when I just manage to glimpse a tree that had fallen across the road, blocking about three quarters of the road, I don't know how but I managed to swerve to the right to get past. *Miracle* We also realised we were totally lost, and I stopped at the first house we came to. I got out and knocked on the front door. The owner answered, and I told him I was lost. 'No, you're not, you're here' he replied, but then gave me directions to get to our destination. A distance of just over two thousand miles.

Chapter 17

Our Golden Year

Our home in Norton Fitzwarren.

Ruth and her family relocated to Calgary in two thousand and eight and after spending Christmas of two thousand and seven with friends of the church, we moved into our new home in the village of Norton Fitzwarren in January two thousand and eight. It's what our North American friends would call a trailer home, here we call them park homes. It is forty-four feet by twenty feet wide, has two double bedrooms, one of which has an ensuite bathroom with a walk-in wardrobe, a separate bathroom, a fully fitted kitchen and an 'L' shaped lounge/diner. It is much more manageable. Another great advantage is I no longer get half way upstairs and then forget what I was going to get, so I would have to go down stairs to get my brain engaged.

Mum and I went to Canada one more time. We flew into Toronto and Clive and Leslie were there to meet us. Instead of heading west to where they lived, we headed East. We drove through the Province of Quebec and stayed a night in Montreal. Clive showed us the house they lived in and where Mo had lived in following Leslie's operation back in the 'seventies. I didn't particularly like the city, too much graffiti and blatant prostitution on offer for my liking. We continued on to the province of New Brunswick and stayed a night with friends of Clive in Fredericton. Our destination was Prince Edward Island (PEI). We were going 'out of season' so we were able to rent a cottage very cheaply. We stayed there three nights and visited Green Gables. Green Gables is the name of a 19th century farm in Cavendish, Prince Edward Island and is one of the most notable literary landmarks in Canada. The Green Gables farm and its surroundings are the setting for the popular *Anne of Green Gables* novels by Lucy Maud Montgomery. The site is also known as Green Gables Heritage Place. The house was designated a National Historic Site in 1985. Mo was delighted. I think she read all of the novels based on the farm. Anne of Green Gables was the first novel and there are seven further books. We bought a small wooden model of the farm house and it sits on the front door step even today.

From here we made our way to Nova Scotia and drove around the island visiting Peggy's Cove which is the most visited and idyllic village. Situated on Nova Scotia's Bluenose coast and the area is renowned for its hiking trails, kayaking and whale watching. We made our way around the coast and reached the memorial to Swissair flight 111, the flight of a passenger airliner that crashed on September 2, 1998, off the coast of Nova Scotia, Canada, killing all 229 on board. The subsequent investigation determined that faulty wires caused the plane's flammable insulation to catch fire.

Finally, we visited the Bay of Fundy, which is known for its high tidal range. The quest for world tidal dominance has led to a rivalry between the Minas Basin in the Bay of Fundy and the Bristol Channel. The Bay of Fundy lays claim to the highest tides in the world. The highest water level ever recorded in the Bay of Fundy system occurred at the head of the Minas Basin on the night of October forth, nineteen sixty nine during a tropical cyclone named the "Saxby Gale." The water level of 21.6 meters (71 feet) resulted from the combination of high winds, abnormally low atmospheric pressure, and a spring tide.

In two thousand and ten we reached our Golden wedding anniversary, and we held a celebration in Norton Fitzwarren's village hall. Our friend, Di Doyle, took charge of the catering, and eventually the celebration cake came out, but where was the knife? It came out of the kitchen carried by Mo's brother, Clive. This was a total surprise to me, but I suppose I only have myself to blame. I had trained my children too well! On this occasion, Julia had invited Clive and had sworn him to secrecy. So, Clive made the first cut and then the cake was taken out to the kitchen to be cut into slices, whilst Mo hugged her brother with tear filled eyes. However, who should carry out plates of sliced celebration cake, but Ruth and our granddaughter Jessee. Lots more tears and hugs and applause from our guests. However, I was still to have the final surprise. I made a short speech thanking everyone present for coming and turned to Mo and said you have just got time to pack, we are off to California in two days' time.

Chapter 18

New Zealand

We did fly out to Los Angeles two days later where we were met by Clive's daughter, Trina. We stayed with her and her husband Mitch for a week. Trina took us to the beach one day and I hired a car and Mo and I drove to Death Valley National Park which straddles the state of California and Nevada. It is the hottest, driest and lowest of the National Parks in the United States. I needed to buy fuel, but the nozzle of the fuel pump was too hot for me to hold so I called the attendant who wore thick protective gloves. The temperatures in August average out at forty-six degrees centigrade. That's hot!

Towards the end of the week I thought I had better tell Mo what was going to happen next. We would be flying on to New Zealand for three weeks. She had longed to visit the country. We flew into Auckland on the North Island and made our way to our pre-booked hotel for the next four nights. We just chilled out the next day but on the following day we take took a coach tour to the Bay of Islands, a three hour drive north of Auckland. We took a boat ride looking for and finding dolphins. We drove back to Auckland and our hotel and the next day in the evening we met with others who were to join a fourteen-day coach tour of New Zealand.

The next day we boarded the coach and had a short tour of Auckland before heading for the Glow worm Grotto which was truly amazing. The next destination was the Pohutu Geyser which spurts several times a day at heights of up to a hundred feet. In the evening we went to a traditional Maori dinner and folk show including the Maori men performing the Haka.

The next day we made our way to Wellington where we joined the ferry to South Island making our way along Queen Charlotte Sound to the sleepy village of Picton. Our next stop will be Milford Sound and a boat tour along the Fiord. We had an unexpected delay while we waited for the snow to be cleared from one of the passes.

We then drove to Queenstown for an overnight stop. In the middle of the night we were rudely woken by the room shaking. An earthquake had stuck Christchurch approximately three hundred miles away. The tour continued and two nights later we arrived in Christchurch and stayed in the centre of the city. We walked around surveying the damage the earthquake had caused which was quite extensive. We were approaching the end of our holiday in New Zealand and we had to catch a connecting flight from Christchurch to Auckland for our flight back to Heathrow via Hong Kong where we had an overnight stop.

Chapter 19

The Worst Day of My Life

The twenty sixth of January twenty thirteen started just like any other day. In the afternoon we went into town and did a little shopping and came home and had dinner and then settled down to watch television in the evening. We watched the ten o'clock news and had supper and decided to retire for the night. I took the mugs into the kitchen. Mo continued on along the passage towards the bedroom and one step past the kitchen door she called out "Phil, I can't breathe."

I rushed out and she had slumped down onto the floor and was leaning against the wall. I phoned the emergency service and spoke to an ambulance dispatcher. I had the phone on speaker, and as I was asked questions Mo gave me the answers to the questions. Two ambulances were dispatched, but by the time they arrived Mo had slumped down on to the floor. The crew gave her heart massage for twenty minutes, but I knew in my heart that she had died. During that twenty minutes I phoned Teresa and told her that there was a problem with Mum and the paramedics were dealing with it and would she tell the rest of the family. She and Hannah were with me quite quickly. Eventually the paramedics stopped, and they took me into the lounge and explained that they would have to call the police, as it was a sudden and unexplained event. They also carried Mo into the spare bedroom and laid her on the bed. I asked Teresa and Hannah if they would put a nightdress on Mo, I know Teresa had done this type of thing during her nursing days, but it was very harrowing for them both, especially Hannah, never having seen a dead person before and now having to tend to her Mother. Because it was a Saturday night the police were busy with the town centre crowds and it was gone midnight before they turned up. Eventually they were satisfied, and I was able to call the undertaker and they took Mo to the Mortuary at Musgrove Park Hospital.

The next few days were a complete blur. Teresa went through the address book and got in touch with everybody. The service was held on the fifth of February at Creech St. Michael Baptist Church by the Pastor, the Reverend Ewen Huffman. I thought there would be about a hundred people there, but I seriously under estimated just how popular and how many people had been influenced by her life. Our immediate family totalled over thirty and the chapel was full with people standing at the back. There must have been over two hundred people there. We had decided to have a willow coffin and I asked my six grandsons, Adam, Stuart, Alex, Christopher, Tim and Sam to be the pallbearers. Tim read Psalm 91 "Whoever dwells in the shelter of the Most High will rest in the shadow of the Almighty." Then I had to share some of our life together. Then followed a musical tribute 'In the garden' played by Mo's brother, Clive and his son Jonathan, and sung by our eldest grandson, Adam. The gospel, singer songwriter and preacher, Marilyn Baker could not attend unfortunately, but our daughter Ruth read out her Eulogy. Finally, Mo's lifelong friend Jennie read from 2 Corinthians 1:3-7 "Praise be to the God and Father of our Lord Jesus Christ, the Father of compassion and the God of all comfort...."

When we wrote our wills, it was my wish to be buried at sea, but Mo wanted to be buried at Tatworth cemetery. I can understand why, as we both looked upon South Chard Church as our spiritual home. After the service we drove to Tatworth cemetery for the internment, but the journey took longer than expected and by the time we got back, most had left and there were many that I was unable to thank personally.

In the immediate days after, I went back to my driving patients to and from hospital. I would work six days a week, sometimes knocking up between four and five thousand miles a week. I had to concentrate on driving, which helped me to get through my days. But I needed something to fill my thoughts in the evenings. I turned to my usual anti-depressant remedy, model making. Over the years I have made intricate models of the Cutty Sark and Nelson's Victory. This time I decided on a table top 'N' gauge model railway. As on the previous occasions I was in a hurry to get started and laid the track and constructed the various buildings and forgot about installing the electrics for the points. I would spend three or four hours each evening in the conservatory until I was thoroughly exhausted and then staggered off to bed. I consulted with my doctor about my depression and he referred me to a bereavement support group that was held in a meeting room of the fire station of all places. He also prescribed anti-depressants, but the possible side effects were so diabolical that eventually I gave the packet to my son-in-law, John who was taking them.

The final thing I needed to do was to change the church I attended. I felt I needed to make a new start. I started attending the nearest evangelical church, which was Kings Church Quantocks, a small fellowship of Christians who met each Sunday in the village hall in Bishops Lydeard, just five minutes away. Very quickly I felt very much at home. Every Sunday I would arrive half an hour before the service and would help 'setting up' the place ready for the service. Afterwards there were refreshments available and also putting the meeting room back to normal. Teresa and Colin started to come and support me. She would arrive with a Costa coffee for me. When John's business failed, and he and Julia could not afford the rent each month, I suggested they should move into my spare bedroom and so they also joined the fellowship as well. Everyone was so welcoming, the Pastor, Brian and his wife, Marion, invited me to lunch on several occasions.

Over time, I got my life back. I no longer needed the therapy of the model railway and gave it away to a single parent in the fellowship who had a young son. Also, I joined a house group that met in various homes on a Wednesday afternoon for bible study and after a while I offered my home as a venue. Eventually Teresa and Colin started a small meeting in their own home with a few folks that needed nourishing. John and Julia moved to Winsham and joined the church, we all as a family had grown up in, South Chard Church!

Chapter 20

But Life Goes On

Even before the funeral I thought, but after the event I shared it with my girls and my church family, that the solution was to put my head in the oven and end it all. But that wouldn't work, my oven is electric. So, life goes on. I had a certain amount of money put away and it was my intention it would be shared out with the five children. However, they all agreed they didn't want it but would prefer good memories, so in the last five years I have been trying to visit as many places on my bucket list and taking one of the girls with me. I have decided to focus on one of the children at a time and write about more than one event rather than do it in a chronicle order of trips.

The first was with Julia. In September twenty thirteen we flew to Toronto, met Clive and Leslie and made our way down to Florida, where Clive had a time share. We drove through New York State and then the States of Pennsylvania and Maryland, I was hoping to visit New York, to visit Ground Zero but that proved impossible, but we did get to visit Washington DC. We broke our journey and stayed a couple of nights in a smaller town just south of the capital and spent a whole day in Washington. We took a tourist coach tour around the important sites like the White House, the Arlington National Cemetery and the stunning architectural buildings on the National Mall. We continued our journey driving through the States of Virginia, North and South Carolinas. The time share had two bedrooms but Trina, Clive's daughter had flown up from Los Angeles which meant I slept of the bed settee. It was so uncomfortable I put the cushions on the floor. The solution was to hire the adjoining apartment. That was one of Clive's lasting virtues, generous to a fault.

We divided our days on the beach, right across the road, and sightseeing; we visited a Crocodile park and took a boat trip to see some of the enormous brutes. As we were leaving Julia spotted a ranger with a two-year-old 'gator and he let her hold it. On another day we drove to the Everglades National Park and visited a historic Indian reservation situated in a swamp area, we walked around the site on raised walkways through the trees to the centre of the settlement and watch native women making native souvenirs for the tourists to buy. The highlight of the holiday was a three-day cruise from Fort Lauderdale visiting Key West and Grand Cayman Island.

Julia holding a 'gator.

I took Julia on a second trip to Norway in March twenty seventeen. We flew from Gatwick Airport to Bergen and transferred to the port by bus. We then transferred to the Hurtigruten ship MS Finnmarken. It is half cruise ship with accommodation for nine hundred persons but is also used as a car ferry and mail ship for the numerous settlements as the vessel makes its way northwards along the coast of Norway.

There are so many settlements, some are missed, and those will be visited on the way back to Bergen. Some stops are for half a day so we can take an optional tour, but some stops are only for twenty minutes or so just to drop of a pallet or two of supplies and perhaps a car and locals returning from a trip to Bergen. We visited Trondheim and went to the Nidaros Cathedral. The city is known as one of the typical wooden cities of Europe and there are wooden buildings dating back to the seventeens hundreds.

On Day five we went ashore at Tromso, 'capital of the Artic.' On day seven we reached Kirkness the turning point, from here we will make our return journey south to Bergen. Bergen is very near to the Russian Border and road signs are in Norwegian and Russian. While we were within the Arctic circle we experienced the thrill of seeing the Northern Lights. The village of Vesteralen is the centre of the cod fishing industry of Norway. There are six buildings, fishermen's huts, and behind them are huge wooden racks. The fish are caught and gutted, salted and dried and these racks and the cod is known as 'flippfisk.' When dried it can be exported all over the world. All to soon our twelve day holiday comes to an end as we arrive back in Bergen.

In May twenty fifteen, I with Julia, Teresa, Ian Gemma and Taya, Hannah and Ian, flew to Mexico, where we met up with Ruth, Graham, Jessee and Sam together with Jackson, Tim's son, who had flown from Calgary for the Wedding of Tim, their eldest son, to Jessica. We stayed at a resort hotel with its own private beach and a variety of restaurants. It was very hot, up to thirty-two degrees so most of the time was spent drinking diet coke in the shade, or in the pool doing aerobics. On one such event I forgot I was carrying my I-phone in my pocket. That was the end of it.

My Next 'Making Memories' was with Hannah in June twenty fifteen. It was a 'flying visit', just a week. We flew into Rome and then she had a bit of a shock. Because of my age I wasn't allowed to drive the hire car. I don't think that up to that point she had ever driven on the 'wrong side' of the road, and here she was confronted with excitable Italians who drive as if every journey is a formula one race. Scooter riders are ten time worse, weaving in and out of other traffic. I have to say she was fantastic. The next day we drove to the Colosseum, the Triumphant Arch which shows the spoils of war taken from Jerusalem, including the Menorah, perhaps better known as the Seven Branched Candelabra. We visited the Catacombs and took an open topped coach tour of the city. A visit to the Vatican. We spent three days in Rome and then made our way south to Pompeii. We opted to give the motorway a miss, so we took a leisurely drive through the numerous small town and villages, so it was evening when we arrived. We drove around the modern town several times looking for the bed and breakfast accommodation I had booked. We had a twin bedded ensuite room, and breakfast was a voucher that we took to a café situated in the main square. We spent the day at the Roman ruins of ancient Pompeii, which is huge stretching to over one hundred and fifty acres. Out of an estimated population of eleven thousand, over two thousand perished, many where they sat or stood, entombed in ashes, which as it cooled became volcanic rock. The next day we drove a few miles north to Naples and the ruins of Herculaneum. After the eruption of Vesuvius in 79A.D. the town was covered by between fifty and sixty feet of ash. It was generally believed that the inhabitants had fled as early excavations did not reveal any skeletons, but twentieth century excavations revealed a group of fifty-five skeletons on the beach, waiting to escape by boat. In the nineteen nineties more than three hundred skeletons were found huddled together in two groups of twelve arches facing the ancient harbour. Herculaneum is a much smaller site due to modern day buildings built around the site. It was time to drive back to the airport, and this time we went on the motorway and it took half of the time. The trip was on my 'bucket list' and it was also on Hannah's list as well, and I really enjoyed spending quality time with her.

Her second trip with me was in January of twenty eighteen. I really felt that a holiday was called for to escape the winter weather. So, she came with me on a two-week cruise around the Caribbean. We caught the train to Gatwick and booked into one of the airport hotels for the night. Next morning, we were up early and took an airport bus back to the airport, checked in and then went for breakfast. The flight was uneventful, and we walked down the steps from the aircraft onto the tarmac and boarded coaches which I assumed was going to take us to the terminal. Wrong, we exited out of the airport at what can only be called the back way, we were on our way to the ship in Bermuda. During the cruise around the West Indies we would visit Antigua and Barbuda, the Turks and Caicos Islands, Sant Kitts, Martinique, British Virgin Islands, Saint Lucia, St Vincent and St. Maarten.

My next 'Making Memories' was with Teresa. We went on a cruise from Southampton to the Baltic in July twenty sixteen. We caught a train from Taunton to Southampton and took a taxi from the railway station to the docks. Our first destination was Copenhagen, the capital of Denmark, then Stockholm in Sweden, Helsinki, Finland. I was impressed by the Temppeliaukio Church in Helsinki. It is a modern evangelic Lutheran church, built in the sixties built directly into solid rock, it is known as the Church of the Rock. The inside walls of the church are just the original rock face, which give excellent acoustics. The organ has three thousand and one pipes and thirty-one stops which admits pressurized air to set of pipes. Outside if you were not aware of the church, you would probably walk strait past it unaware of what is inside the rock. Light comes in from the glass panels that surround the roof just over the dome. Today, however it is one of the most popular tourist destinations in the city with over half a million visitors a year and is a popular venue for concerts. We also visited the central market and had lunch in a tented food outlet, I chose a sausage meal made from reindeer and Teresa opted for Elk. When we left to make our way to the coach, the heaven's opened. I have never been in a storm like it, within minutes the road became a river, but we had to get back to the coach as soon as possible, soaked to the skin.

The next port of call was St. Petersburg, which was the highlight of the trip as far as I was concerned. We first went on a coach tour and stopping every so often to get off for a more detailed explanation from the guide. Then we went on a boat tour on a canal, and I remember how rough the waters were. We sailed passed the Peter and Paul fortress, founded by Czar Peter the Great in seventeen hundred and six and took over forty years to complete. After the Bolshevik revolution, it was used as a prison and execution ground, but now it has been developed as part of the State Museum of Saint Petersburg. I had difficulty in reconciling what I was now seeing to my memories of Kharkov when I was there in the nineteen nineties. Our final port was Tallinn, the capital of Estonia. The Old Town is very picturesque and is listed as a UNESCO World Heritage Site and has over sixty museums and galleries. Our tour visited the Old Town and we walked through the narrow-cobbled streets. We returned to the ship and made our way back to Southampton where friends of Teresa met us and drove us back to Taunton.

That just leaves Ruth and Ian. I am meeting up with Ruth and Graham in September in New York City. It has been on my list of places to visit ever since I didn't get there in twenty thirteen and it has been on theirs as well. We plan to visit Ground Zero, and just around the corner St. Paul's Chapel. Enjoy a meal at the Marriott Marquis hotel's revolving restaurant seeing the sites of New York. A visit to Ellis Island and the Statue of Liberty is also a must. Then for the second half of the week we are hiring a car and driving up to Boston and Philadelphia to learn a more of the Boston Tea Party and the early settlers to North America.

Ian retired from the Police Force in August of this year, and we will have to sit down and plan a memory.

Chapter 21

My Health

In the last two decades I have had a few rough patches, health wise. I have type 2 diabetes which I am managing quite well. I have to inject insulin, but over the last couple of years I have managed to reduce the dose from thirty-two units a day to sixteen. Mo was worried that it would limit our excursions, but it hasn't stopped me at all. More serious was a prostate cancer diagnosis in two thousand and five which led to a radical prostatectomy. In twenty fourteen I was admitted to hospital with pneumonia and inflammation of the gallbladder. I was re-admitted later that year to have the Gallbladder removed, but on investigation the surgeon found that my appendix had moved and was now sitting on top of and joined to the gallbladder, so there was no option but to remove both organs. Just as well because the appendix was infected as well. I still can't work out how that happened!

In twenty sixteen I had an endoscopy investigation when it was discovered I had Bowel Cancer and had surgery to correct that. I have just had a further investigation and given a clean bill of health. In July tweny seventeen I had been in Calgary for the wedding of Hannah to Ian. Ruth drove me to the airport and I went through the security check OK, but realised I had left my walking stick on the counter. I wasn't allowed to go back so took a seat while I waited for it to be brought to me. It was then then I felt a bit woozy, but I boarded the aircraft. For a once in a life time trip, I upgraded my seat to first class. As soon as we were airborne I had an orange juice and promptly went to sleep. I missed the meal trolley, the drinks and duty-free trolleys and woke up as we were flying over the Bristol Channel. An hour later the plane was landing at Gatwick airport. I caught the train to Reading, where I had to catch the train to Taunton. Teresa was there to take me home. It had been a long trip and as soon as I got home on the Saturday evening I went to bed. I woke at four in the morning with an unbearable pain in my right shoulder. I phoned 111 emergency line and an ambulance was dispatched to take me to Musgrove Park Hospital. I was very quickly taken from the emergency department to the Cath lab. I couldn't understand what six or so staff were doing just standing in the corridor, they were the surgical team waiting to operate on me. I had had a heart attack and the shoulder pain was the indicator. How was I to know that a pain in my right shoulder was caused by a problem in my heart. I had a single stent inserted through the right wrist and spent the next four days in the hospital recovering. *Miracle* I went through an eight-week rehab course which monitored my recovery, but more importantly gave me the opportunity to examine my aims in life.

Although I was a committed Christian, it was always Mo that led, and I followed. She tithed, I did occasionally; Mo read her bible every day, I read it occasionally. However, I knew without any doubt that I was a servant to which ever church I belonged to. I was a Deacon. Now I decided I had to be more committed. I started to tithe and set up a banker's order, so that where ever I happened to be, my gift would be paid. I started reading the Bible and Christian books. This led to my researching the Bible and writing sermons, just for pleasure, with no expectations of delivering them. I would share them with Teresa who would proof read them and give me suggestions how to improve them. Then I would print them off and file them away in a ring binder. Now find I have got a regular preaching spot four times a year. Never saw that as part of the plan.

Chapter 22

The Bucket List

Colin and I at the Garden Tomb.

In April twenty fourteen, Colin, my son-in-law, and I went to the Isle of Man. We drove up to John Lennon Airport, Liverpool and flew to Douglas. We booked into a bed and breakfast on the sea front.

One of the interesting things I noticed was the squares of patched tarmac in the road. This was where the security fence had been erected during WW2 for the internment of German Nationals. I presume it would have been in this area that my niece's German father would have been interned. We bought a three-day pass which gave us unlimited journeys on the trams and narrow-gauge trains. We made good use of it, first travelling from Douglas to Port Erin in the south of the Island. The next day we took a longer trip to Ramsey in the north of the island. On the third day we experienced the Snaefell Mountain Railway, which is an electric operation and uses an incline railway on the steeper sections as the summit is just over two thousand feet above sea level. The line starts at Laxey which is where the Laxey Wheel is situated. It is seventy-two feet six inches in diameter and was used to power the mines because the Island has no coal. Because both Colin and I were bus drivers, we also made a point of visiting the Transport Museum at Jurby in the north east of the Island. Soon our holiday was at an end and it was time to make our way back to the airport and flight to Liverpool.

Then in November, he and I went to Israel for a week. After landing at Tel Aviv we took a sheerot taxi to Jerusalem. This is a seven-seater taxi and you pay for a seat and it only goes when the vehicle is full. When we got to Jerusalem we went on a mystery tour through narrow streets dropping people off at their front doors and we were the last two to be dropped off at the Rivoli Hotel, an Arab hotel in Salah Eddin Street in East Jerusalem, where I had booked us a twin room. It was so convenient for visiting the Garden Tomb, the Western Wall and the Temple Mount. First, we went to the Western Wall and from there we went on a tour to the Temple tunnel. What we see today is some two hundred feet above ground, but a further sixteen hundred feet has been excavated down to the bed rock and starts at the corner stone or Western Stone, which is forty-four feet long, ten feet high and an estimated width of eleven feet with an estimated weight of five hundred and seventeen tonnes. We eventually reached street level near the Ecce Homo Convent on the Via Dolorosa which is the traditional route Jesus carried his cross. The next day we entered the old city by the Dung gate and joined the security queue to go onto the Temple Mount. Today it is where the Golden Dome stands, completed in A.D.691, but originally was the site of the Second Jewish temple, which stood on the site from 516 B.C. until it was destroyed by the Romans in A.D.70 during the Jewish revolt against Rome. The Garden Tomb was very meaningful for both of us. The site was excavated in eighteen sixty-seven. General Gordon visited the site in eighteen eighty-three and it was he who put it on the map. I have been there many times, but I still feel the sanctity of the place. On one of the trips I led our tour for an evening stroll. We walked along the wall of a garden and I mentioned that the Garden Tomb was on the other side. We met a party of Jewish soldiers on patrol and I greeted them in

Hebrew. As it was Friday evening I said, 'Shabbat Shalom' which means 'have a peaceful Sabbath.' They wanted to know if I was Jewish, so I had to explain that I was a Christian who loved Israel and it's people. This led me to showing the Star of David that I wear around my neck. This is a very special one I had especially made for me on one of my visits to Jerusalem. In the middle of the Star of David is the Christian cross, so I can explain that what supports the Christian faith is the roots of the Jewish faith. If Judaism fails, so will Christianity. On the top each arm of the Star of David is a Lion, representing the tribe of Judah and on top of everything is a Crown, representing Jesus, the Christ.

The next day we hired a car and made our way to Jericho. We stopped at the Inn of the Good Samaritan. On previous visits I have always had to point out that it is only a parable, but excavations started in the late nineteen nineties and it has been proven to be the original Khan, or Inn, that had been rebuilt in the Temple period, the Byzantine, Crusader and Ottoman periods. We stayed with an Arab family in their home in Jericho. That was a new experience, but Arab hospitality is very genuine as it is in the West Bank, Egypt or Libya. The home was beautiful and gives an insight to some of the Palestinians still living in refugee camps in the West Bank. The garden was filled with grape vine, date palms, orange, lemon, lime, fig and pomelo trees.

We made our way north but stopped at Beit She'an for an hour at the ruins of the important city at the junction of the Jordan River Valley and the Jezreel Valley. A settlement began five thousand years ago but it is the ruins of the roman period that we see today including the public toilet. A long bench sited along a wall with a series of holes where you could sit and do your business and converse with your neighbour, be they male or female. It wouldn't be for me. So, after this we continued on our way to Tiberias, and we stayed at a hotel just south of the town. The good thing about it was there was a secure parking compound at the rear. The next day we visited places so familiar with the ministry of Jesus Christ; Capernaum, the home of Peter; St Peter Primacy, where Jesus charged Peter to feed His sheep;

The Mount of Beatitudes where Jesus delivered his Sermon – 'Blessed are those who......'

Our penultimate day was spent visiting Nazareth and Mount Tabor, the site identified as the place of the Transfiguration. We then made our way to Haifa and stopped at a view point overlooking the city and the Temple of the Bhai faith. Their adherents' faith is similar to that of Muslims, but the tenants of their faith are secret and handed down generation to generation. The final place we visited was Caesarea Maritime which was the chief city of the Roman administration. Concerts are still held in the Amphitheatre because of the superb acoustic properties due to the prevailing winds blowing eastward toward the audience.

In between these two trips, Mo's lifelong friend and prayer partner, Jennie, accompanied me on a cruise along the Rivers Rhine and Danube. These two rivers dominate Europe and are joined by the Rhine-Main-Danube Canal. We flew to Passau where we boarded the boat for our fourteen-day trip. We would sail through Germany, Austria, Slovakia, Hungary, Serbia, Bulgaria and Romania. We visited Vienna, Budapest, Belgrade and some smaller towns as well. When we were in Budapest we took a coach trip to the Lazar Equestrian Park show. The journey ended at Constanta on the Black Sea coast where I dipped my toes into the water.

I did a couple of solo trips in twenty sixteen. First to Ironbridge, over Easter in March twenty sixteen. I drove up on the Friday and booked myself into a small hotel on the main street overlooking the River Avon. The town of Ironbridge is named for the first Iron Bridge made in seventeen seventy-nine. The museum is actually ten different museums spread over the region and include the Blists Hill Victorian Town. I started at the bank and changed a ten-pound note for shillings and pence. And bought fish and chips for one shilling and a penny, six pence in today's money. There is also a tile museum and a china museum. Then there is the Coalbrookedale Museum of Iron and the Museum of the Gorge, which has a model, which is twelve metres long, of all the various sites. The home of the Darby family built in seventeen seventeen and Rosehill House give an insight into how life went on in the period. I didn't know what to expect at The Broseley Pipework's, but it certainly was clay pipe where you can see the actual pipes the men used to smoke. But I think what I enjoyed the most was the Enginuity museum, where you can pull a ten-ton locomotive single handed, using a series of wheels and pulleys.

In October twenty sixteen I took a rail trip up to Western Scotland and the Inner Hebrides. I boarded the train in Taunton and headed for Fort William. The holiday was arranged by Pathfinder Tours. We were served with Lunch and afternoon tea on the train and then when we arrived at our hotel where we were served dinner. For the next three days we toured the region by coach. The scenery is spectacular, the roads were narrow especially for a coach. Just as well that the traffic was light, most times car drivers pulled into a passing point to let us through. We had crossed to the Island of Mull by ferry, but the high light for me was the visit to the Isle of Iona, which we crossed as foot passengers. In the year five hundred and ninety three Saint Columba and twelve companions, having been exiled from Ireland, founded a monastery which played an important role in bringing Christianity to the Picts of Scotland. All to soon it was time to make our way to the railway station for our return journey. We found our seats and sat and sat for the next four hours or so. Because rail tracks in this part of Scotland are single track, so when an engine becomes derailed everything comes to a halt until the incident can be resolved.

In November twenty seventeen I joined Operation Christmas Child as a volunteer. A year before I responded to an appeal to help collect shoe boxes from all-over Somerset. I thought it was a very worthwhile enterprise. Churches, schools and individuals fill shoe boxes for less privileged children in Eastern Europe and Africa. As the volunteer had retired at the end of twenty sixteen I took over the roll for the year twenty seventeen. I had a team of four other volunteers and over the next four weeks collected five and a half thousand shoe boxes. I had the opportunity to join a team to fly out to Albania in December to distribute just a few of the four thousand shoe boxes that were sent to that country. I needed to raise seven hundred pounds. I prayed for the balance needed to go to Albania. One lady gave me five hundred pounds and a couple gave me the other two hundred pounds. *Miracle* Seeing their faces light up you would think we had given them the world.

Albanian children with their shoeboxes.

Finally, in twenty eighteen Teresa and Colin took me on an eightieth birthday treat to Slimbridge Wetlands Trust. It is a place that has long been on my bucket list. Two weeks before I asked her if we could take my grandson, Tony along with us, no she replied, this is our birthday treat. I dropped the idea and thought no more about it. We got to Slimbridge at about ten thirty in the morning and parked up, and the three of us hung around in the carpark while Teresa lit up a cigarette. I thought it was better to have the smoke in the car park so I quite happily waited. Then I noticed Julia and John walking towards us, then Ian and my granddaughter Taya, and his two boys Chris and Alex, with his fiancé Harriet. Gradually it dawned on me, Teresa had pulled the ultimate surprise on me. Apparently, she had been working on this for the last year. With John and Julia there was Adam and Stuart, with his wife Katie and their two boys Daniel and Jono and their fostered teenage girl; Hannah and her husband Ian and her two boys, Tony and Nat; and the biggest surprise of all, Ruth had flown in from Calgary just for the weekend. We followed this up on the Sunday by all meeting up at a local pub for a carvery lunch, before they all dispersed, to Heathrow, Leeds, Sutton, Plymouth, Hereford and Dorchester. It will be some time before they can repeat such a surprise.

I have come to the end of my story, who knows what the future holds. That is the trouble of writing an autobiography, but I have enjoyed it immensely.

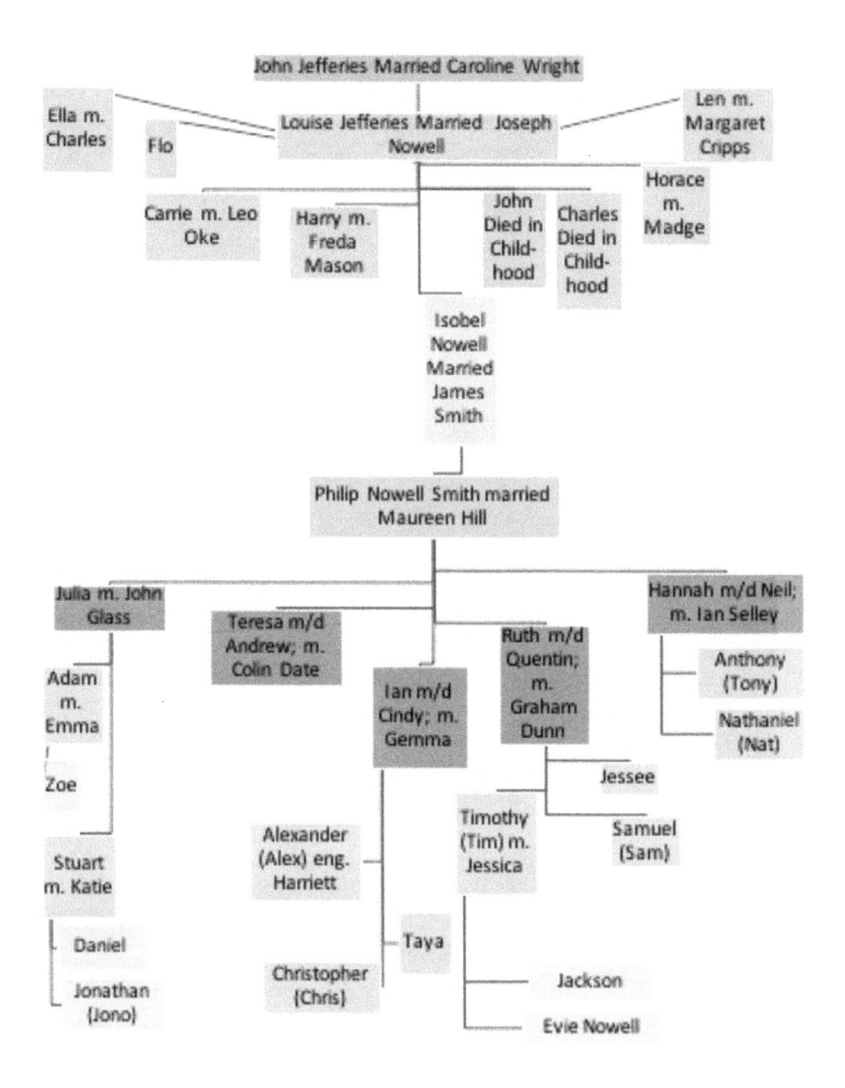

```
                    John Jefferies Married Caroline Wright
Ella m.                  Louise Jefferies Married  Joseph              Len m.
Charles      Flo                     Nowell                          Margaret
                                                                      Cripps
                                                    Horace
            Carrie m. Leo   Harry m.   John    Charles   m.
                Oke          Freda   Died in   Died in  Madge
                             Mason   Child-    Child-
                                      hood      hood
                           Isobel
                           Nowell
                           Married
                           James
                           Smith

              Philip Nowell Smith married
                      Maureen Hill

Julia m. John                                              Hannah m/d Neil;
   Glass                                                    m. Ian Selley
           Teresa m/d                  Ruth m/d
  Adam     Andrew; m.                  Quentin;              Anthony
   m.      Colin Date                     m.                  (Tony)
  Emma                  Ian m/d        Graham
   /                    Cindy; m.       Dunn                 Nathaniel
  Zoe                   Gemma                                  (Nat)
                                              Jessee
                                    Timothy        Samuel
  Stuart              Alexander     (Tim) m.        (Sam)
  m. Katie            (Alex) eng.   Jessica
                       Harriett
  Daniel                                  Taya
                                                   Jackson
  Jonathan            Christopher
   (Jono)              (Chris)                     Evie Nowell
```